M000199993

3

Dear Aileen,

Know yourself

And choose Love

well.

To Your Success in
" finding Your Love
At Last ",

Dr. Renée

Praise for

FINDING YOUR *Love* AT LAST

"What you teach is so valuable. Everyone in the world should have a copy of your book as their go-to love and relationship guide-book."

— Dr. Wayne Dyer, Author of
Your Erroneous Zones and *Manifest Your Destiny*

"Brilliant! The author walks her talk. Too many books talk about the subject of love from an academic position. Finally, here's an author who has gone through heartbreak only to learn from it and put it into a step-by-step guide to finding love success."

— Eric Lofholm, President and CEO of Eric Lofholm
International and Author of *Sales Scripting Mastery*

"Finding Your Love at Last will not only motivate and inspire you; Renée Gordon will show you what not to do as well as how to find Mr. or Mrs. Right!"

— Dr. Ava Cadell, Founder of Loveology University and
Best-Selling Author of *Neuroloveology*

"It's about time to read a book on relationships that tells it like it is! The timeless information in this book takes you step by step through a practical love discovery process that makes lots of sense."

— Adam Markel, CEO of New Peaks, Best-Selling Author of
Pivot: The Art & Science of Reinventing Your Career & Life

"If you're in search of a soulmate, someone to spend the rest of your life with, this book is for you. It offers simple truths that have the power to profoundly alter how you view lifelong loving relationships."

— Susan Friedmann, CSP, International Bestselling Author of
Riches in Niches: How to Make it BIG in a small Market

"If you're looking for the relationship of your dreams, this book is the best place to start."

— Patrick Snow, International Bestselling Author of
Creating Your Own Destiny and *Boy Entrepreneur*

"Renée Gordon has found the perfect five-step process for finding lasting love. In this book, she will teach you how to separate Mr. or Mrs. Wrong from Mr. or Mrs. Right, watch for red flags, and find someone truly compatible to be your soulmate. The world has been waiting for this book!"

— Tyler Tichelaar, Ph.D. and Award-Winning Author of
Narrow Lives and *The Best Place*

"Your soulmate may be the most important relationship in your life, and Renée's book clearly outlines the steps to finding that special person. If you're currently looking for your life partner or plan to in the near future, this book is for you!"

— Nicole Gabriel, Author of *Finding Your Inner Truth*
and *Stepping Into Your Becoming*

"After reading and re-reading Renée Gordon's book, I think of Love at Last as the place where science meets love! Renée is one clever woman. She tells you exactly how to find the 'needle in a haystack!' She uses the best skills found in business and science to hone in on what and who matters and obtain extraordinary results! Few people have the organizational skills, tenacity, and bravado to create a process that Gallup would love for finding the perfect match that can lead to a lifetime of solidarity, love, and fulfillment in a marriage. Because Renée has done the work, she speaks credibly about her process while she makes it easy to reproduce her results. Her honesty, coupled with her insight and experience, make this a must-read book for anyone ready to stop guessing, stop wasting time, and stop floundering through traditional methods of finding someone you can trust and love."

— Jimm Hughey, Business and Relationship Coach and
Author of *Delightfully Married!*

"Once in a while, a very rare and special soul comes forward, dares to change the status quo, and creates a new and revolutionary way to make a dramatic change in our lives. Renée Michelle Gordon is that person! She has created with divine inspiration a beautiful way to attract our true special mate in sixty days or less. Finding a soulmate is about loving, caring, sharing, support, happiness, and being with not only the love of your life but your best friend as well. Finding Your Love at Last demonstrates this principle and will help you achieve it. I highly recommend this book. It will literally change your life!"

— Dr. Michael Gross, Professional Keynote Speaker, Life Coach,
Entrepreneur, and Author of *The Spiritual Primer*

"We live in an age of superficial clichés about dating and hooking up, when people all too often rely solely on apps and algorithms to find romantic happiness. Here, finally, is a work of real practical value to help us cut through the noise. Finding Your Love At Last is a serious and systematic plan that anyone can use to grow self-awareness and identify for the first time the values and qualities he or she truly prizes in a soulmate."

— Stan Freeman, Attorney-at-Law

"A simple step-by-step guide that will have your ideal soulmates lining up to date you."

— Curtis Phelan, Curtis Phelan International

"This book is a revelation, a breakthrough reframing of how we think about ourselves and how we approach one of the most important decisions in our lives: choosing a partner for life. A must-read for those in search of a nurturing, joy-filled, long-term relationship."

— Brett Watson, Paralegal

"Renée Gordon's book, *Finding Your Love at Last,* is a must-read for those dating and those already in a relationship. Many books give love advice, but this book uses stories to explain the necessary steps, then encourages and inspires the reader to take them."

— Deborah W. Ellis, Author of *Achieving Financial Security*

"Having just ended a long-term marriage, my radar for relationship discovery was in need of serious renovation. Renée Gordon was a true find. Her ideas, suggestions, and guidance were instrumental in my selection of Mr. Dreamy—my current and best relationship ever. I couldn't have done it without you, Renée. I highly recommend this incredible book and amazing woman."

— Tamra Nashman-Richardt, CEO of Extra-OrdinaryImage

"Fun, inspiring, and motivational. You'll never look at dating the same."

— Lynda Lamp, Author of *Walking Through Your Walls*

"At last! A relationship book that actually has a foolproof system to attract the love of your life. Renée is brilliant! Her proven process is guaranteed to bring in your soulmate in ninety days or less!"

— Arvee Robinson, International Speaker and Author of
*Speak Up, Cash In: How to Use Speaking
as a Marketing Strategy to Attract High-Paying Clients*

"I was blessed to know Renée before she found her 'Love at Last.' I was amazed by the discipline and thoroughness she took when she started to put her plan in action. She did possess the qualities needed, which were being loving, responsible, driven, motivated, and of high moral character. It didn't surprise me that she found such a wonderful man who fits like a glove. I have no doubt that following the exact steps of this plan will work for anyone who is ready, willing, and able to take the next step."

— Lecia Westerman, Real Estate Investor and Entrepreneur

"This fantastic book, *Finding Your Love at Last,* is spot on. The lessons that Renée Gordon teaches are simple and easy to follow."

— Kevin A. Dunlap, Professional Speaker and
Author of *Designing your Own Destiny*

"Have you ever wondered what the missing success link is to having and achieving a loving, nurturing, and caring relationship? You'll find it in this book."

— Karina Tangwulder, Author of *Climbing Your Route to Success: How to Unleash Your Passions to Achieve Your Dreams*

"This is a terrific book that all single people should read before they get married. It's a great guidebook to navigate to finding your love at last."

— Mike McDole, Author of *Creating Your Greatest You*

"Divorce would be obsolete if everyone had a copy of Renée's groundbreaking book. Who knew that my own values would determine who was right for me? I'm giving a copy of Finding Your Love at Last to all of my single friends to ensure each of them will have a happy relationship like I will."

— Renee Merlo, Co-Author of *Trade Secrets to Designing Your Life*

"Bravo! And, finally, an author who gets it. It's not about a pretty profile picture on a dating website. But rather, it's about attracting someone of matching principles. This book is destined to become the go-to relationship guide."

— Irene K, Co-Author of *Trade Secrets to Designing Your Life*

"Finding your love at last has simplified and clarified what's important to me; I'm excited and feel confident that my next relationship will be the one that lasts."

— Kim Phuong Dang, Author of
Drifting Lotus, Spirit of Survival

"Thank you, Renée. I was thrilled to work with you. You made my coaching sessions fun and impactful. I was married for twenty-two years and had a painful divorce. You said it may take a little while to step into my authenticity and really know myself. Your process was so powerful and motivating that I found my 'Love at Last' within ten weeks of working with you. You are a master and genius at helping people find their true love. I'm now married and have a new baby girl. Thanks to you, I'll always be indebted."

— Craig Minnett, Food and Wine Expert

"I have seen Renée Gordon mesmerize audiences with her passionate work on relationship success and true happiness. Now she gets to do it for others everywhere by bringing her expertise on to the pages of this wonderful and informative book. When I first met Renée, I was truly a work in progress, but as a life coach, she helped me to find my way, to be honest with myself, and so much more. I am so honored to have met her. She has been such an inspiration to me. She has accomplished so much in her life. She will change your life with her love, enthusiasm, and optimism."

— Denise Carroll, Animal Communicator and
Author of *What Is Your Pet Telling You?*

"Renée Gordon, author of Finding Your Love at Last, has helped me by giving me the tools and support for finding love. Renée has been so inspiring and knowledgeable in the area of relationships. After being divorced three times, she has shown me how to attract the right person and write down in detail what I am looking for. I have learned so much from her and her book.... Thank you, Renée, for being such an amazing friend and support to me in finding love and knowing what I want and deserve!"

— Karen Dafesh, Beauty and Skin Specialist,
The Skin Connection

"If you've been holding your breath to find that special person, you can now sigh in relief. Congratulations! You are on your way!"

— Gaylyn Kinnett, Real Estate Entrepreneur

"If you're going to run through a minefield, you had better follow someone who made it through. It takes a plan to have the love of your childhood fantasies, and Renée's wonderful book, Finding Your Love at Last, gives you the footprints to follow as you search for your true love without a disappointing ending. Don't be afraid to follow a leader to get what you truly want."

— Michael Kinnett, Real Estate Entrepreneur
and Molecular Hydration Specialist

"A great guideline for everyone in any phase of his or her personal relationships. Interesting, informative, and well-researched."

— Tom, Real Estate Entrepreneur

"This amazing book is the result of Renée learning the key to life's lessons regarding love, attraction, and finding the right partner. She has remarkable insight and fierce determination once she accepts the challenge of finding out who you are and then the best fit for you. Finding Your Love at Last is insightful and full of helpful ideas for locating that companion who makes you a better person."

— William E. Collins, Attorney-at-Law

"Having had the pleasure of knowing Renée Gordon personally and watching her evolution in life for many years, this is a determined woman who practices what she preaches. And she doesn't settle. Unlike me, she didn't have three divorces by age thirty-eight. She admittedly learned from her earlier misfires, skipped time-consuming weddings, didn't waste her emotional bullets on divorce court, sought out expert advice, and developed her own proven and successful process for finding the love she wanted and deserved. Her goal was to dance the Hula and Tahitian dance for her "one and only husband," and that's exactly what she did. I know this for a fact because I sat with a sizable group of her remorseful ex-boyfriends at Renée and Jim's wedding reception, and all they could talk about was that they were jealous Renée wasn't dancing for them! She set her sights on the highest goal and danced a very beautiful hula for the man who won her heart. She knows what it takes to find and receive that type of love, and she shares it here with you. Read on and find the love that's meant for you."

— Constance-Noelle Hatley, ACS, ALB, Life Coach
and Author of *Heart Languaging*

"Renée is definitely an expert and your go-to gal in the area of long-term relationships. Renée has spent countless hours putting her expertise into a book to help those searching to find their true loves. The timeless information in this book takes you, step by step, through the love-discovery process. I am proud to say that I have learned so much with this book that I, too, will find my love at last."

— Christina Ramirez, Founder and CEO of A-1 Gate & Entry

"Some people talk about relationships from the outside looking in. This book is in a class of its own, beginning with a testimonial from Renée's spouse. Next, Renée takes an internal look at her own life—her mistakes and lessons learned—and then embraces herself for a quest to find answers for not only herself but others as well. Get off the sidelines and move to the front of the pack. This is your book for finding that lasting and loving relationship."

— Professor Rosalyn Kahn, Coach and Professional Speaker, Author of *Random Acts of Kindness Are Changing the World*

"*Finding Your Love at Last* is an eye-opening book into the real life of dating. Renée has captured the true feelings that go into finding your soulmate and offers her tips to help you on your journey to find true love. Truly a heartfelt read."

— Amber Borbon, "Body by Amber" Master Pilates Instructor

"The search for love does not have to be complicated in youth, nor does it have to become perplexing in maturity. Having a simple, yet thorough process, as laid out in Renée Michelle Gordon's book, is the lifeline we have all been seeking."

— Josef Schein, Disc Jockey/Master of Ceremonies, Danse Forté

"Renée is by far one of the sweetest people I have met. She is there to help others succeed in so many ways, but her heart (and her heart is bigger than she is!) is really there to help you find your 'Love at Last' or spice up your relationship if you already have. Like her 'Love at Last' husband, Jim, who also has an incredible heart, has written, he had a wonderful wife, but she was the wrong lady for him. I also had a wonderful husband, but together we were wrong for each other. I have dated some wonderful (and not so great) men in my journey through my life, but have not found the right person for me. I am looking forward to Renée's teachings to help me find my 'Love at Last.'"

— MaryLou German, Hair Stylist
and Business Entrepreneur

"Wow! I can't wait to share *Finding Your Love at Last* with my clients and friends who are longing to attract the perfect soulmate. I'm confident if they follow Renée's simple five-step process, they will experience a dynamic and transformational journey to passionate, committed, and amazing love."

— Dr. Rita Dumas, LMFT, Ph.D.,
Reconnect to Success Coaching Center

"Renée's candid and honest insight on finding your true love is refreshing. She's given me hope that I will find my soulmate and live the life I've dreamed about with him. After my divorce, I wasn't so sure, but now I'm excited about the possibilities. Thank you, Renée."

— Sandy Sinden, Travel Authority

"Renée Michelle Gordon writes from the heart and with passion and honesty.... This book is a sensible and clear-cut way to look at love and how to find the love of your life. Step-by-step processes and easy reading make this book a must for anyone who is looking for love and being successful."

— Julia Cantu, Team Leader and
Independent Consultant, Apriori Beauty

"Renée Gordon gives us permission and encourages us to be ourselves. Such a basic and beautiful concept, however, is often under-emphasized by our society and social media. A big thank you to Renée Gordon for sharing her recipe for finding love and keeping it spicy."

— Melisa Nusbaum, JSG Insurance Services

"If you are looking for your one true love, this is the book you need! Renée's five-step system has helped hundreds find their soulmates. Now, with this astonishing book, she is sharing her secrets with you!"

— Susie Fabrocini, Author of *Making Your Finances Fun & Sexy:*
The Do It Yourself Guide to Financial Planning

"After reading the first few pages of Renée's book, I was encouraged by her words of wisdom to help me keep my twenty-year relationship fresh, new, and exciting."

— Alisa Altman, Keller Williams Exclusive Properties

"I'm a married man so I don't remember much about the single life, but many of my friends and people I lead every day are always asking for this type of advice. So what do I tell them? Get a copy of this book and let Renee Gordon share with you how to find your soulmate."

— Matt Jenkins, Author of *Becoming A Great Leader*

"Renee is a self-made woman! Whatever she wants she tends to get. She is extremely giving and has a heart of gold. Renee likes to help people see more for themselves and achieve it. She has opened my eyes to many things, love included, through her creative, pragmatic, and well-disciplined thoughts and plans. I admire and respect her."

— Holli Hume, Principal, Pacific Financial and
Insurance Services

"Renee's advice on how to find a loving relationship is priceless. It is practical, insightful, and uses a sensible approach to finding what we all want in life."

— Judy Gordon

"*Finding Your Love at Last* is an amazing book and I feel that Renee is one of the leading experts when it comes to finding new love as well as enhancing and sustaining the current love you have. I was so thrilled to see that she starts the book out with helping readers understand the importance of knowing yourself and knowing what you want. Thanks, Renee, for the wisdom tips and love strategies you shared from your heart and experience...you rock!"

— Raven Blair Glover a.k.a. The Talk Show Maven,
Award-Winning Radio Host and Former CNN Correspondent

"When you're ready to stop making the same dating mistakes over and over, read this book. Dating is a skill like any other. Learn how to do it right, once and for all, from the woman who wrote the book!"

— Dr. Sharone Rosen, Chiropractor

"Renée's heart of gold and spirit of generosity fill the pages of this book. Her life experiences have clearly shaped her sense of purpose and given true value to her advice and lessons."

— Hamilton M. Carsen, Author of
Finding the YOU in YOU-unique

FINDING YOUR *Love* AT LAST

FIVE SIMPLE STEPS FOR
ATTRACTING YOUR SOULMATE
WITHIN 90 DAYS

RENÉE MICHELLE GORDON

Interviewed by Peter Lisoskie

Foreword by Jim Connolly

AVIVA
PUBLISHING
New York

Finding Your Love at Last
Five Simple Steps for Attracting Your Soulmate within 90 Days

© 2016 Renée Michelle Gordon

Published by:
Aviva Publishing
Lake Placid, NY
(518) 523-1320
www.AvivaPubs.com

All Rights Reserved. No part of this book may be used or reproduced in any manner whatsoever without the expressed written permission of the author. Address all inquiries to:

Renée Michelle Gordon
www.FindingYourLoveatLast.com

ISBN: 9781943164950
Library of Congress: 2016951173

Editor: Tyler Tichelaar/Superior Book Productions
Cover and Interior Layout Design: Nicole Gabriel/Angel Dog Productions

Every attempt has been made to source properly all quotes.

Printed in the United States of America

First Edition
2 4 6 8 10 12

Disclaimer

The purpose of this book is to educate and entertain. Neither the author nor publisher guarantees that anyone following the ideas, tips, suggestions, techniques, or strategies within it will become successful. The author and publisher shall have neither liability nor responsibility to anyone with respect to any loss or damage caused, or alleged to be caused, directly or indirectly, by the information contained in this book.

Dedication

To my father, Jim Gordon, who is in heaven with God. I am immeasurably grateful to you. I love you and thank you for your undying love and belief in me. You taught me that I was born to be anything I wanted to be. You gave me your generosity, philosophy of personal and business life skills, and the incredible teachings of "street smarts" that I needed as an adult. You are always in my thoughts and prayers. I will always be grateful to you.

My father taught me the importance of positive values and to have strong ethical beliefs. He showed me how to be resilient, how to deal with challenges, and how to strive for excellence in all I do. He taught me that there's nothing I cannot accomplish if I merge vision and passion with a persistent and focused work ethic. One of my father's greatest talents was the ability to see potential in people before they saw it in themselves. It was like that for me growing up. He taught me that potential vanishes into nothing unless you make an effort.

And like my father, I have a responsibility to my work, not just for myself but for the betterment of the world around me. When my father was in charge as a leader, his results said that all that counts is ability, effort, and excellence. He would say to me "Sweet Pea, if you're going to be thinking anyway, you might as well think big. Don't be afraid to set lofty goals and be relentless and determined to achieve them."

"Fall in love with someone who doesn't
make you think love is hard."

— Unknown

Acknowledgments

"In the end we only regret the chances we didn't
take, the relationships we were afraid to have, and
the decisions we waited too long to make."

— Lewis Carroll

No book is written by itself, and so I wish to thank the following
people for their wonderful support:

To my remarkable and inspiring husband, Jim, for his love, patience, persistence, wisdom, and strength. If it weren't for him, this
book never would have been written. Thank you, God, for sending
him into my life. I cherish and appreciate every moment we are
together.

To my "children." Even though God did not bless me with human
offspring, I've been blessed with the four-legged and winged variety of dependents. Thank you Jean-Luc, Lord Bentley, Joy, Harmony, Bliss, and, of course, Kiwi for the continuous joy you have
brought me and for filling my soul with love.

To my mother, Christmas, for giving me life and the motivation to
be successful with that life.

To Yvonne, for being my sister and inspiring the artist within me.

To Auntie Joy Abbott (Mrs. George Abbott), who taught me her
distinctive sense of style, elegance, and panache, and more importantly, to achieve timeless feminine beauty inside and out.

To the memory of Dr. Wayne Dyer for his inspiration and encouragement that he gave to me to complete this book. I am honored to have had him review my book and say, "Everyone in the world should have this as a love handbook."

To Dr. Barbara De Angelis, thank you for your years of encouragement and inspiration and for recognizing the similar path we both travel.

To Dr. Ava Cadell for your friendship, love, support, and continuous encouragement in my becoming a love and relationship authority like you. I strive every day to make you proud.

To Adam Markel, for your transformational, motivational, and inspirational teachings and for showing me how to make those "pivots" in my life to create that "slight edge" for my success.

To Peter Lisoskie, for helping me in the preliminary development of this book and for the interview format that makes it real to the reader.

To Patrick Snow, my business mentor, speaking, and media coach. Thank you for your generous daily wisdom, encouragement, philosophy, and belief in me.

To Nicole Gabriel, you took my vision and created a spectacular book cover. You made this process so simple and easy. You are a unique graphic designer with an artistic eye for creating an image that matched the title of my book so perfectly.

To Tyler Tichelaar, the Wizard of Editing, you made completing this book less daunting. I appreciate your patience; you made me feel so special; I always felt as though I was your only client. You have superb skill. Your speed and accuracy is unbelievable.

To Les Brown, thank you so much for your encouragement and speaking coaching expertise. I've learned so much from you and have taken to heart your quote that I live by, which is, "Stay HUNGRY!!!!"

Thank you, Terry Ledbetter; you are my brother from another mother. I appreciate all of your support and love throughout the years. You are the physical manifestation of the many values and beliefs that my father, your friend and mentor, holds dear.

To Dr. Michael Gross, who has helped me in so many ways and is continuing to help me connect with "God, the true source" of authenticity and truth.

To Tom and Sue, Real Estate Entrepreneurs, thank you for being that example of how a working couple of over thirty years can continually love, respect, and nurture one another. I learned that and much more from you both.

To Jimm and Susan Hughey, whom I lovingly call my "two love birds." Thank you for your continual support and being the example of finding your love at last too.

To Michael and Gaylyn Kinnett—wow, the original power couple, your continual love, support, and example of how two intelligent entrepreneurs can effortlessly come together to work, live, love, and play is an inspiration to both Jim and me.

To Tony Robbins, Lisa Nichols, Adam Markel, Dr. John Demartini, John Assaraf, T. Harv Ecker, Marcia Weider, Marianne Williamson, and Eric Lofholm, thank you for being my mentors and sharing with me your wisdom and expertise. My transformation would not be complete without all of you.

To Donald Trump, in those years that I worked with you, you impacted my understanding of what it takes to be a success in business.

Thank you to the hundreds of people who have entrusted me with helping them find their own love at last. It is because of all of you that I am committed to helping all of those people who have yet to find their soulmate and to give them all hope that it is not only possible, but probable for them to find their own Mr. or Mrs. Right because you, my students, have proved that it does work. I have learned so much from you all, and I am humble and in gratitude to call you my friends.

And most of all, thank you, God, the source, for giving me my life again a second and third time in order for me to complete my life's purpose—to share my knowledge and experiences and to help so many others in "finding their love at last."

Contents

Foreword

I have the honor, privilege, and delight to be the recipient of Renée's amazing process for finding "Love at Last" because I am the one who got to experience it for the first time and firsthand. I'm Renée's husband. I get to share with you my experience going through her process of "Finding Your Love at Last: Five Simple Steps to Attracting Your Soulmate Within 90 Days!"

I've never met a women in my life who is so creative, intelligent (and street smart), personable, inclusive, loving, and mysterious (yes, even to this day!) as Renée. I thank God every day that I am married to her. Then I thank God for the five-step process she created that allowed us to find each other. I know if it wasn't for this process, we would have never found each other or enjoyed the life we have together.

But before I explain to you about Renée's love-finding creation, please indulge me as I share with you my love story. Like many of you who are experiencing this program, I had been previously married to a wonderful woman. And she still is a wonderful woman, but she was not for me. You see, as wonderful as she is and was to me, some of our core values and beliefs were very different. We loved each other very much and were blessed with a phenomenal son Christopher. But love was not enough. Even my son could see that after we split to become two households. He understood that our breakup and later divorce were best for everyone involved.

At first, after our breakup, the last thing I wanted was to be in another relationship. I resisted the temptation to latch on to another person out of loneliness. Remember, the loneliness did not start right after our divorce was final; it had started in the years that led up to our initial breakup. As much as I yearned for the companionship of another woman, I was wise enough to know that I needed to work on myself first before I brought another person into my life. You see, I was fortunate enough to realize that the one common denominator in all of these issues that contributed to my breakup and later divorce was me. I was at the center of all of those issues, so I figured I better get my own head and heart on straight before I began another romantic relationship.

The time I spent between divorcing my first wife and meeting and subsequently marrying my sweetheart was twelve years! This journey of self-discovery was the greatest gift I could have given myself to prepare for the love of my life. Could I have been ready sooner? Sure, but I had no guidance or direction to pursue to make that happen. I guess I could have devoted myself to only the pursuit of the love of my life, but I didn't. I spent years redesigning my life to have the life I always dreamed of and deserved. So when I was ready for my life partner, I was really, really ready.

Many of you probably did what I did when you decided it was time to find Mr. or Mrs. Right. You told your friends, you put yourself out there through your network, or you gambled on the open market online. Maybe you joined some dating groups that hooked you up with more singles than you could shake a stick at! I had some success. But for the most part, most of my relationships lasted no more than three months tops! I had one relationship that was officially one year long and unofficially two years in length (that is another whole story in itself!) None of my searching produced anything concrete enough to be considered real. Oh, I was engaged very, very briefly during what my son and best friend considered the day an alien took over my body. That relationship was like a shooting star; it burned bright and poofed out of existence almost as quickly as it came. So nothing real until....

It was late April or early May 2000. A girl friend of mine (unromantic girl friend) was having a hard time finding the right guy for her. Being a good friend, I offered my services as an unbiased set of "guy eyes" to check out her profile page. She called her profile page, "Are You the One for Me?" the title of Dr. Barbara De Angelis' book, which I had given to her. So I proceeded to search her out. She was on Match.com, and even back then, it was one of the largest online dating services on the web. In the process of searching for her profile, I noticed an interesting profile just above my friend's titled "Ex-Model/Chef." Well, that profile headline got my attention because it was short and seemingly conflicting (little did I know then how accurate it really was and how not conflicting). Well, because I was professionally trained as a chef, even though I wasn't doing it as a career at the time, I was curious to take a peek at whom this person could be. I mean, after all, the title seemed contrary to itself. A chef likes food and usually likes to eat well, whereas a model avoids food to keep her physical shape in check. I had to see this person. Little did I know that would be the beginning of something life changing and also the beginning of the Love at Last process for me.

Yes, you guessed it; I had coincidently stumbled onto my future life partner's profile page! Remember, it was the headline that got my attention, and then I got to see her obviously professionally-produced picture of her and her canine companion of seventeen years, Bianca. Renée was attractively dressed in a unique outfit of zebra stripes with matching hat and boots. *Stunning*, I thought. And she was posed like a model for a magazine shoot—very elegant. I was impressed! But what really made me take action and write to her was reading her profile. It wasn't made up of the usual silly crap that I would read from other people looking for their love interests. You know what I mean, the "Let's hold hands on the beach," or the "Are you my soulmate?" BS. She was real; this woman knew what she wanted, and more than anything else, she knew who she was to the world. She struck me as a very confident woman, which is very sexy to me. So I didn't hesitate; I wrote her a message I won't share with you right now. (I'm showing a bit of mystery in me, too. But I promise I'll share it with you in one of our live workshops or membership learning academies.)

Renée and I talked on the phone for two to four hours every day for six or seven weeks! It was obvious we had a connection. The challenge was she lived in Beverly Hills, in Southern California, while I lived smack in the middle of Silicon Valley, Northern California in San Jose—a good five- to six-hour drive or one-hour plane ride away. Finally, I flew down to see her. We met for brunch at a luxury beach hotel, and we haven't been apart since. But it was Renée's process that brought us together and has kept us passionately connected to this day.

Now that you know my side of our story, let me share with you why this process of finding the love of your life even exists for you. It wasn't until about six or seven years ago that I found out how we had really met and that I was actually a part of a process that was created by my sweetheart years earlier. Yes, I had heard the stories about the nine wonderful guys she had been engaged to in the past. But I had never given any thought to how we had found each other until she shared it with me that day. She explained the five-step process she had created for herself because she was tired of attracting great guys who were wrong for her.

When I realized the challenges I had gone through in my search for my own love at last, I said, "I wish I'd had this process when I was looking for my life partner. With all of the time and money I spent looking, dating, calling, and breaking up, I would have spent anything, done anything to get the results I now have. When I was ready to find the love of my life, I wanted to learn what was necessary and to take the proper actions to get me to my Mrs. Right in a path that was more of a straight direct line. Of course, now that I had found my Mrs. Right, I didn't need her program, but many people like me will be giddy to know they can have a process to help them find what I have found—a relationship with someone who fits, who matches so well that you look forward to waking every day to continue your journey together. So I encouraged my sweetheart to help other people—as she had helped us—to find their own love at last!

So with the birth of Love at Last, through her coaching and teaching processes, Renée has helped hundreds of people find their own one true loves. She has also helped these couples re-commit to the passion they have with each other when most relationships become stale and tired. She is passionate in helping people discover the core values and beliefs that drive them to building the best relationships they can possibly have and to pursuing their missions and purposes in life together. Now Renée is ready to take what she has been doing individually for the past seven years for real people just like you and share it with the world through this book, her online love academy, her live relationship boot camp, and, of course, her Finding Your Love at Last: Five Simple Steps for Attracting Your Soulmate Within 90 Days! workshop and personal one-on-one coaching.

By the way, the name of her love and relationship coaching business, Love at Last, was created because we know that the love and relationship we both found was not just for each other, but within ourselves. So Love at Last is all about the creation and discovery of the love that we each have first with ourself, then with our life partner, then with our community or tribe of friends, family, and colleagues. Love at Last is the yearning we all are looking for in our lives that makes us feel accepted and loved unconditionally. So, like a parachute, which only works when it is open, do the same with your mind and heart as you experience this process. Open your mind and heart so you really see, hear, and feel the message that is right just for you. So with all of that, I'd like to introduce my love at last, my Mrs. Right, my life partner and best friend, Renée Michelle Gordon. Please enjoy the process and have fun in your own journey to the love of your life!

With all of my love, hope, and anticipation,

Renée's "Love at Last," Jim Connolly

Preface

You'll see that most of this book is written in a conversational style because it was a dialogue between my friend Peter Lisoskie and me. Besides being a good friend and mentor, Peter's encouragement to complete my book has been invaluable. His knowledge of the latest in neuroscience has contributed to my understanding of the complex relationships that we have with our life partners. He believes, as I do, that love starts with yourself first before you welcome someone into your life. Also, that knowing yourself, your values, and your beliefs is the foundation upon which to build a long and loving relationship with your Mr. or Mrs. Right.

Peter's interview expertise as a talk radio host on his show *Home Matters* has been used in this book. He plays the role of you, the person looking for your love at last—your soulmate with whom to share a life together. This format makes reading *Finding Your Love at Last* easy to read so you feel like you're listening in on a conversation between friends at a local Starbucks.

Peter is also the creator of the Croc Brain Selling System. Through his understanding of the latest neuroscience research, he has exposed the wrong ways we've been speaking to the buying brain. In addition, he's the owner and creator of Inviral Academy, a product and marketing incubator that quickly takes products to market. You can visit his respective websites at www.crocbrainselling.com and www.inviralacademy.com.

I am honored to have Peter play the role of interviewer in my book to help you, the reader, better understand the Love at Last five-step process for finding your soulmate and life partner.

Thank you, Peter, for all of your help.

Of course, if at any time while reading this book, you, the reader, get excited about finding your love at last and would like to do it at a faster pace than by just reading this book, call me directly at 424-281-0170 or email me at Renee@FindingYourLoveatLast.com to ask about my many coaching packages that will help you accelerate your own love search so you don't waste another day alone.

Finding Your Soulmate!

You're tired of going to weddings by yourself, or even worse, scrambling to find a date to be your "plus-one" only to find out that the person is a "zero" or "less-than-one"! You're frustrated at being the only person among your friends to attend every major event by yourself from parties and birthdays to holidays and other special occasions. Your idea of an exciting weekend is being surrounded by your pets while you binge-watch last season's episodes of *Empire* or *Game of Thrones*!

Are you looking for that special person who will be your best friend, your lover, your Mr. or Mrs. Right, your love at last? Are you ready to share a life with someone who adds color to your currently black-and-white existence? Are you willing to do what it takes to make it happen—to find your love at last?

Look, I understand what it's like. I was once like you. I was that person who hosted many dinner parties as the only single person in a room of happy couples. When asked whether I was seeing anyone, I'd say, "Oh, I have plenty of dates and people who take me out, but I don't want to introduce them to my friends because they aren't special enough."

But who was I fooling? I wanted what my couple friends had—a someone special with whom to share my life.

You may be a single parent or working two jobs. You may still be in pain from a previous bad breakup or divorce so you feel a bit gun shy about putting yourself out there again. Or you may have had the courage to do it again, so you ventured out into the world of online dating, only to be once again disappointed because you attracted the wrong type of person or you met those people whose pictures are from when they were fifteen years younger, twenty pounds lighter, or still had a full head of hair!

Here is the good news; you are holding in your hand the same five-step process that helped me find my love at last. I've experienced what you've experienced, and if I can find that special relationship in my Mr. Right, so can you.

This simple five-step process has been tested by over 500 couples just like you who thought that they too were relegated to being alone for the rest of their lives. They followed the same process that is in your hands now, and they found their love at last.

Each step takes you closer to finding your love at last. The first step will be the foundation to everything else you will do. It's about Knowing Yourself. This step sets you up for success; it was my missing piece and the missing piece for most of the people I have coached.

Step Two is Knowing What You Want. Now that you know who you are and what values and beliefs you hold dear in your life, you're better able to determine who is the right person for you.

Step Three is Attracting Mr. or Mrs. Right. Learn the reason why you keeping attracting that wrong person into your life and recognize that person before you make that mistake again. Then figure out how to attract the right person.

Step Four is Knowing Where to Find Your Mr. or Mrs. Right. Where are the places to find your love at last? I'll share with you physical places and situations that put you into a great environment for attracting your soulmate as well as how to find your Mr. or Mrs. Right as I did, from an online dating website.

Step Five is Choosing Your Soulmate and Finding Your Love at Last. This step is where everything is brought together, and I'll share with you how to interview your love prospects without them even knowing it's an interview. By this time, your confidence will be at an all-time high, and that's the best place to be to make the right decision on who is right for you.

If you follow the steps in this book, do the homework, and stay focused, you too could find your love at last and do it in ninety days or less! I know that once you realize you're done wasting your time being alone and that now it's time to live fully, you'll be in a hurry to get to your special person. Therefore, this five-step process is designed to get you what you want in ninety days or less. But if you're more of a process type person, you can take your time. Whether you do this process quickly or take your time, you'll be confident that you're heading in the right direction for you!

You're probably asking yourself, "Why, Renée, should I listen to you? What makes you the expert who can tell me how to find my Mr. or Mrs. Right?"

Well, as I said earlier, I was just like you, attracting the wrong people into my life, going to weddings, birthday parties, and other important events by myself. Heck, I was even engaged to be married nine times, only to come to my senses and call each one off before I made a bigger mistake and went through with each wedding.

Then I realized that the only thing each unsuccessful marriage engagement had in common was me. So I began my journey of focused discovery in personal development. I learned from the relationship masters: Dr. Barbara De Angelis, Dr. Wayne Dyer, Dr. Ava Cadell, and many others. They became my teachers, my mentors, and my friends. I spent tens of thousands of dollars and many hours of study and reflection to put together this five-step process to help me find my love at last. And I did! Of course, I did it so well that I attracted over 2,874 people at first before I refined my search system to attracting that one person who was right for me.

Once I did attract the right person, my single friends began asking me to help them with finding their own loves at last. Then their friends asked for help, and then the friends of their friends did the same. To date, I have now helped over 500 couples find their life partners, and I can help you too.

I know you're probably thinking that this process sounds like a lot of work, and you don't know whether you have the time to do all of this searching. Do you realize that most people put more effort into planning their one-time vacation than they do into attracting a life partner?

Yes, some focus is required to find your love at last, but I promise you, if you follow my simple five-step process, you will quickly be on your way to finding the relationship of your dreams. I did most of the work for you. I've spent the time developing a system that is focused on getting you to Mr. or Mrs. Right. You just need to follow along, feeling confident that this time you'll be making the right choices.

So if you're ready, I'm ready to be your love coach, your dating advisor, your relationship mentor, and your guide in helping you find your love at last. If I can go from nine failed marriage engagements and being alone on weekends with no prospects in sight to finding my love at last, then you can too!

So are you finally ready to find your love at last? Are you ready to learn more about who you are and who is the right person for you? Are you ready to end a life of solitude and begin to live life with your soulmate? Are you ready to gain the confidence that, once and for all, you have control over what is right for you? If you are, let's get started. Let's do this journey together, and once and for all, let's find your love at last!

CHAPTER 1

Knowing Yourself

"Do not lose yourself in the process of treasuring someone too much and forgetting that you are special and valuable too."

— Author Unknown

"Open your arms to change, but don't let go of your values."

— The Dali Lama

Knowing yourself is not just imperative for finding the love of your life; it's critical for all areas of your life! Most people don't take the time to self-evaluate who they really are, and after all, how do you expect to find the love of your life if you don't know yourself first? Building your new relationship with someone special without knowing yourself first is like building a home on a poor foundation that could collapse at any time. In this chapter, you'll learn that your values are the building blocks to knowing who you really are. Those building blocks contribute toward your Love by Design™ process that we will discuss later. You'll also learn that interests and hobbies are only secondary when finding your life partner; they are the sprinkles on top of the sundae, not the ice cream itself. Understand that by clarifying your values and beliefs, you are 80 percent closer to finding your love at last.

Why is it so important to know yourself before starting to look for the love of your life?

What makes values so influential in your decision-making process when looking for Mr. or Mrs. Right?

What's the difference between values, beliefs, interests, and hobbies?

Let's dive into this chapter and listen to my interview with Peter. Peter and I will talk about the importance of knowing yourself within the process of finding the love of your life!

Peter: To begin, Renée, maybe you can tell us your story. How did you come to be a relationship expert? What happened to you in your life to cause you to develop this book and program?

Renée: For me to find a boyfriend was pretty easy. I've always had a boyfriend or boyfriends. I had boyfriends I'd date here and there—lunch, dinner, cocktails—but I wouldn't necessarily be intimate with them if I were dating different people at the same time.

Finding a boyfriend was very easy. Before I did online dating, I was engaged nine times with a ring, a wedding date, and even deposits with a contract at some of the most elegant ballrooms in the Beverly Hills area. The Hotel Bel Air, The Four Seasons Hotel, and the Beverly Hills Hotel. I was definitely committed to the sanctity of marriage.

Peter: It sounds like you were committed to the process, but not committed to understanding whom you really wanted.

Renée: Yes. I was attracting the wrong people. They were all very wealthy multimillionaires I was attracting, what most people would think was a home run in finding Mr. Right. But they were wrong for me because their characters, beliefs, and values didn't match mine. Before I would make it to the wedding date, I'd start to think we just weren't connecting on a deep emotional level, and that was incongruent with how we were living our lives.

Peter: That got you thinking there's a better, different way. So what did you do to stumble upon this better way to find the love of your life?

Renée: I looked in the mirror and thought these guys were great on paper, but not great in my heart. They weren't connecting with my inner vibration of who I was and whom I was ultimately looking for. I was listening to my gut intuition, and that little voice that was saying, *This doesn't feel right.*

Instead of going through with it, and then getting divorced nine times, I thought about who was in the center of all these people, who was the common denominator? I looked in the mirror and said, "I'm attracting the wrong men in my life. Why? So I did an extensive amount of work on myself in the areas of personal development and relationship building with many of my mentors to come up with this process for finding the love of my own life. I knew that if I kept looking for the love of my life the way I had been, I'd be attracting the same people whom I didn't want to commit to long term! I needed to come up with a different way to find the love of my life that really worked!

Peter, I also want to remind you that I've created five successful businesses for myself, so I thought about what actions and ideas I had found to build those successful businesses and how I could apply them to finding and having a successful relationship with my Mr. Right. So I created a project of looking for a husband like I would when starting a business, and that began my journey to finding my own love of my life.

Peter: You kind of created a relationship plan, so to speak.

Renée: Exactly, a relationship plan for me. I knew I would find the love of my life, and now I use that same plan to help hundreds of other couples find each other.

Peter: The key thing is whether you're hearing that little voice inside you saying, "Something's not quite right." I guess that's where you were at when you said, "*I have to do something differently if I want to find the love of my life.*" That's very important, and you bring up a great point. I totally get that, Renée. That's super-awesome.

You went through this plan and found the right person for you. But how did you go from helping just yourself to helping others?

Renée: After I met my soon-to-be-husband, Jim, online, we didn't get engaged so much as we decided after 9/11 that it was time to get married.

Peter: You didn't decide this for Jim?

Renée: No.

Peter: That's a good thing. I'm glad it was a mutual agreement.

Renée: He said he knew I was *the one* on the very first date we went out on together. But I wasn't sure because there were so many people I was meeting online. Before I met Jim online, 2,874 men had emailed me. Through some of my strategies, I had a lot of follow up to do before I knew I was sure.

Peter: Oh, geez! How in the heck did you keep track of all those guys?

Renée: I'm going to present later in this book how to keep a journal with copious notes on each person.

Peter: You'll have to share your journal with me some time. I'd be fascinated to read some of your entries.

Renée: It is interesting. In the journal are the people I went out with for coffee, Jamba Juice, lunch, breakfast, etc. I didn't go out with them so much for dinner because that's a two- or three-hour time commitment that I just wasn't ready to make for them yet. I did reserve a dinner or long brunch for a very few suitors who impressed me as being strong candidates.

Peter: You went through this whole process and you found Jim, the love of your life, and you got married. So how did you take your plan and your process that we're going to be talking about and apply it to helping other people?

Renée: I'm going to use my girlfriends as an example because they saw what came into my life. They'd say, "How did you do that? He's so different from the nine other guys you were engaged to; you both really seem to click with each other."

The nine other guys I had been engaged to were all great guys. In fact, they had many similar characteristics, values, and beliefs, including being very wealthy, to the tune of $20 to $65 million or more. In fact, I think the highest net income of one of them was over $72 million in assets! Their bank accounts were extremely high, which was great because security is a very important value for me, but not the only value.

I thought, *Okay, so that's what they have in common. But what am I really looking for?* So I went deep down within myself and wrote about fifty pages of a very specific manifestation letter to God with all the attributes I wanted instead of what I didn't want.

Peter: I see what you did. But getting back to my question, how did you help other people? How did you get this whole business started? You said you started helping your girlfriends and you took them through this process. So what happened for them?

Renée: They got married, and they're living happily ever after.

Peter: Very cool!

Renée: But the ones who didn't follow the process have a lot of problems in their relationships. My friends who were stubborn, didn't want to listen, and wanted to be right are divorced now. Some of them even have kids.

I said, "Now you're married and you're stuck. I pleaded with my friends not to have children with someone they didn't want to spend the rest of their lives with. But they had kids, and five years later, they're saying, "You're right, Renée; I shouldn't be with this guy. But now I have a child." You're committed for life when you have a child.

Peter: Whether you're married or not, you're still with that person through the child.

Renée: Right. When a child is involved, marriage doesn't make a difference either way.

Peter: I guess what you teach in your plan and process is very important. Because it's priceless if you can take a person to find the love of his or her life on the right path, and not on the wrong path where he or she will end up having a rocky marriage or a child. So that's very good.

So you helped your girlfriends, and then what happened next? You mentioned people had heard about you and started contacting you. Is that correct?

Renée: Yes, that's exactly right.

Peter: People were finding you, so what was that dialogue all about?

Renée: The dialogue was with friends and some family of my girl-friends I had connected with who were happily married, and some friends of theirs and family, so it was men and women of all different ages and professions—simply anyone who was ready to find his or her own love at last.

I shared with them the same process I used to find my own love, and I coached them through the process, step by step. I shared with them the pitfalls of what almost everyone does—quickly put together a profile online and hope for the best. I had them commit to the process that first starts with them understanding who they are and what values and beliefs are important to them.

I'd say, "I'm not going to go online with you and pick and choose for you." I'm not a dating coach or matchmaker in a sense that this guy and that girl look great together. My coaching clients are empowered with my process and my relationship-building information. It's up to them because they're the ones who are going to get married—I'm not going to marry them. I'm not a matchmaker per se, but in this process, I've gotten to know people pretty well.

Peter: We're going to talk about this in the book as well. But from what you've told me, this process isn't just about finding your perfect mate. You've also worked with people who want to revitalize their marriages as well. Is that correct?

Renée: That's correct.

Peter: Tell me a little bit about that. How do you help people with your process who are already married?

Renée: I've helped many people who have already been married for over twenty or twenty-five years or longer. Or people who have been living together in a relationship ten years or more.

When you're in a relationship that long, it can sometimes get a little stale, whether sexually or just in the day-to-day monotony. I give them a little advice and consulting about how to add spice to their married life.

Peter: Now I want to ask a question that I think is a great way to get started before we dive into the different chapters of this book: What would your advice be for someone who's looking for the love of his or her life or a couple who is looking to reignite their relationship?

Renée: One piece of advice I would give is to really know yourself, what your purpose is for living on Earth, and why you're here in this existence.

Peter: Why is knowing yourself so important and powerful?

Renée: You need to know what your drive is in order to live a purposeful life and to find your mate—your ideal person—to share your life with.

Peter: I understand what you're saying. Like with my relationship now, it's not only about finding a best friend to have a relationship with, but finding someone you're truly connected to.

Renée: You want to find your best friend because that's who you're going to be with the majority of the time. It's not your boss or your associates if you're working in a corporate office or whatever business you might have, but the person you come home to at night and share your bed and experiences with.

You want to be with your best friend so you can share stories about what happened during your morning, your day, and during the weekends—not necessarily just taking walks on the beach, but being with that person while reading a book or having a cup of coffee, or even not saying anything. One of the best connections is non-verbal because by just being with that person's energy, you feel and vibrate with each other.

I'm going to backtrack. When Patricia, your special sweetheart, opened the front door the first time, you probably stood there thinking, *Wow! She's phenomenal. She's fabulous. She's everything I want.* And then you kissed her.

Peter: It took her by surprise, but I did kiss her.

Renée: You felt that vibration as soon as she opened the front door. The energy, in which she lived, her sanctuary, was the vibration you felt. If it hadn't been right, you wouldn't have kissed her. You would have said, "Hey, let's go for a cup of coffee and I'll drop you off at home." Instead it was, *How many hours can I spend with this beautiful woman of my dreams?* I'm sure on that first date you didn't want to leave.

Peter: No, I didn't. I wanted to stay. That's a great way to kick off this first chapter.

You had mentioned the advice about really knowing yourself, so I have to ask, "Why is knowing yourself such a key element in finding your ideal partner? What is it about that?"

Renée: Finding the right guy or lady takes more than luck and tenacity. Sure a little hard work is a requirement for any successful relationship, but you're much more likely to succeed if the love of your life is a phenomenal long-term fit for your life goals. There's a popular saying, "When you find the love of your life, you'll never want anyone else for the rest of your days."

The most successful relationships often start with someone you're passionate about. And to find a fantastic match that is congruent to your values and beliefs in the world, you've first got to look inside yourself. By knowing yourself, you'll be much more likely to find that special someone who makes you happy for the long term. But more important is to be happy within you first. You are not looking for someone to complete you; you are already complete. You're looking for someone to complement you. In fact, both Jim and I had the same revelation the day before we connected online. We both said, "I'd rather be alone and happy than married and miserable."

It's knowing the foundation of who you are as a person, so you've got to start with yourself first. Where most people get in trouble is they perceive themselves one way when they're really another.

It's very much like building a house on a rocky, unsecured foundation. No matter what the house looks like, the foundation, the essence of that person, isn't on concrete. For instance, if a woman thinks that all it takes to find Mr. Right for her is to make some physical changes to herself like getting her lips and boobs done, that's absolutely wrong. Yes, she may find lots of men who would be attracted to her, but not necessarily the type of man who will be with her through thick and thin.

Instead of spending time and resources only on external frivolous extras, spend some of that money on either a really good personal development program or a coach so you can purge and get rid of all the emotional baggage you've collected throughout your life. Remember, "A Band-Aid will not cover up those emotional bullet wounds from your past." Start brand new on a clean slate so all that baggage won't be brought into your next relationship because, otherwise, you'll carry that baggage with you wherever you go. Start with knowing who you really are before you outline whom you'd really like to be with in your life.

You might be thinking, "Maybe I'll move to another town like New York or Miami and start over fresh; then I can find my life partner there." But wherever you go, your emotional baggage will always follow you. If you don't first like yourself and embrace who you really are, how do you expect someone else to do so?

Peter: It's interesting that you talk about that because it's true. Like you said, spend money on the motivation and personal development instead of the plastic surgeon, so that makes a lot of sense to me (although it is nice to be good looking). But focusing on how you look doesn't lead to that true connection, so I totally understand what you're saying.

Renée: It's what you need to do for everlasting love. But not for a one-night stand, or a few months here and there, or a weekend boyfriend or girlfriend, meaning he'll take you away for the weekend. He's not going to introduce you to his family, but he'll introduce you to his friends to show you off as a trophy. He's just looking to have a weekend fling.

Peter: That's probably the difference between lust and love, right?

Renée: Exactly. There's sex and there's making love. Anybody can have sex. But making love with somebody you're really connected with from the depth of your heart—that's worth the effort of finding the love of your life.

Peter: Going back to knowing yourself and working on yourself first, I guess that starts with your values and beliefs. Why is that important? And then can you explain the distinction between your values and your beliefs?

Renée: You can go on all these different online dating sites where you can slap together a profile and put up some pictures. I understand how tempting that may be, but going back to what I said earlier, if you keep doing what you've done, you'll keep getting what you've always gotten! But if you don't first get right that foundation of knowing yourself, it's like throwing spaghetti against a wall and hoping something sticks. If I had not taken the time to know who I was first, and then to know whom I wanted in my life, my first and only attempt with online dating on Match.com would have been awful. From April to September of the same year, I received 2,874 emails from men on Match.com who were attracted to my profile. I'm not telling you this because I want to impress you; in fact, the reason I'm telling you this is because if it weren't for my beginning love process, I would have been overwhelmed with that many requests from interested men. And even though they may not have taken the time to read my profile and know what I was looking for, I was crystal clear in what I wanted, so the elimination process was made much easier. But I knew that among all of the email requests I was getting, someone in that bunch would be right for me.

I only wanted to find maybe five or six guys to choose from, so when I put up my profile and was immediately swamped with requests, I refined my process some more. It made me think I had to tighten what I wrote in my manifestation letter so I could fit the most vital information into the then required 120 words maximum. So my profile was carefully analyzed, and each "and," "an," "but," etc., was put in and taken out.

Peter: But before you got to that point, you defined all this other stuff that was happening underneath it. Chapter 1 is "Knowing Yourself," so going back to values and beliefs, why is it important for people to know themselves before they define what that other stuff is?

Renée: Let me tell you what I feel the distinction is between a value and a belief by using the metaphor of driving a car.

You're going down the street, and you see the balloons and bright lights of a car dealership. You go into the dealership and see a car and think, *Oh, that looks good!* But you haven't gotten your credit score, and you have no idea how much you have in your bank account. You don't even know whether this car will fit into your lifestyle. But it's a new car and it's tempting to buy. How can you make an important decision like buying a car without first knowing whether you even have the means to purchase a car, what car suits your lifestyle, and what car suits your likes. Does that make sense?

Peter: Yes, that makes sense. So applying that then to values and beliefs, in your mind, what is the difference between a value and a belief?

Renée: A value is the foundation of who you really are, and it's the basis for how all of your decisions are made and how you see the world. Your values become the filter through which you see, hear, and feel the things that come into your life. Therefore, how you live your life is first determined through your values.

For the sake of this book and our training program, the distinction is that a value is a stance that defines who you are and whom you've decided to be. A belief is a reflection or the action you take that represents those values. So a belief can be adjusted or changed, depending upon the experiences you have and the current information you hold about that belief.

Peter: In other words, if you have a value to be a healthy person, but your action is you buy Twinkies, potato chips, and junk food, you really don't believe in that value. Correct?

Renée: Correct, and to add to that example, in January when people make New Year's resolutions to achieve improved health, gym memberships usually go up. By the time March 1 rolls around, attendance goes down, but memberships are still high because people are paying the monthly fee. If your value is health (which happens to be one of my top values), but you decide to do unhealthy things (excessive drinking of alcohol, sitting on the couch all weekend, eating a lot of carbs and fattening foods, etc.), which cause you to weigh 300 pounds, take prescription medications, and be out of breath going up a short flight of stairs, you might want to review health as one of your top values. You see, if you truly value something, it's non-negotiable. You are your values through the decisions you make and the actions you take.

So I am committed to my fitness regimen by working out two hours everyday from 6 to 8 a.m., five or six days a week (Pilates, the treadmill, fitness boot camp, CrossFit, and yoga). My value and actions are then congruent because health is one of my top five values. Not only am I working out, but Jim is juicing for me every morning. So he supports me in my value of health as well because he knows it's who I am.

Peter: Yes, he's helping you with your health values.

Renée: He's washing all the vegetables in alkaline water. He takes the time to make delicious juice smoothies for me with coconut milk and coconut oil, blueberries, and all the wonderful super-greens. I've been drinking that for a few months, so my fitness level and energy have gone up.

I just wanted to mention that if people were healthier, they'd be less depressed and wouldn't need anti-depressants. They would benefit if they'd eat clean, whole foods from the earth, instead of processed, packaged foods, or things in plastic, or restaurant food. And definitely not fast foods. And by being healthy, you have more energy and a more positive outlook on life that benefits you greatly in finding the love of your life.

Peter: So could you give us the distinction between values and beliefs as it pertains to the example of health?

Renée: I'd love to give you an example. As I said a few paragraphs ago, if you have the value of health in your top five or six values, then you'd talk and read about health, do things that would improve your health, surround yourself in your home and office environment with things that had to do with health, and spend money on things that involve your health. If health is one of your values, it's non-negotiable; it's a part of who you are to everyone, especially yourself.

Now a belief could be connected to your value; I'll use the example of being connected to your health value. The difference between a value and a belief is that it becomes a belief through your knowledge and experience. A belief is somewhat negotiable. Here is the example: Let's say that your belief is that all carbohydrates are not good for your health. Then through updated scientific research and reports, you find out that all carbohydrates are not created equal; some are actually very important to your overall health while others can be eaten less frequently. Now a new belief has begun to take shape, so where before you wouldn't touch any carbohydrates, now you have specific carbohydrates that you firmly include within your diet.

Peter: Could you extend this health example to include interests and hobbies too?

Renée: Certainly, Peter. Imagine you had a hobby or interest in riding bicycles, so you ride as an option to support your health. You meet a person who also values health as one of his top five values, but he is more of a runner than a bicyclist. Is that a deal breaker? Well, for me, it's not because it's more important that the person values health and puts it into practice than how he puts it into practice, so running instead of riding a bike is totally okay for me. In fact, because my value of health trumps my interest in riding bikes, I'd be open to running more to provide some variety in supporting my value of health. So you now see why it's so important to know your top five to six values and the hierarchy of where they lie on your list.

Peter: Thank you for the distinction between values, beliefs, interests, and hobbies. Could you expand a bit on the hierarchy of your values before we move on?

Renée: Sure. Say for instance that your number one value is health and your partner's number one value is God/spirituality, and on Sunday morning, you're going on a long bike ride that will take four or five hours, so there is no time to plan anything else that morning. And imagine your significant other wants to go to Sunday morning service with you; well, that may cause tension in that relationship when one wants to go to church as a couple and the other for a long bike ride in the country. Looking at your other values and their hierarchy may help you decide how you solve this issue.

Peter: To tie in to the relationships aspect of values, let's say a woman who values and wants communication finds a young hunk who doesn't say more than two or three words in a sentence. That's probably not a good connection between values and beliefs.

Renée: That's just a boy toy, or a human vibrator.

Peter: There you go! I like that. That's good.

Renée: Maybe it's important for a woman or a man who is fifty-five or sixty years old to find a twenty-two-year-old who can't talk or put two sentences together and has nothing between his or her ears (not that there are not a lot of men and women who are very smart at twenty-two).

But if a way older guy is just looking for a body with nothing between the ears, then after a little while, because there's no conversation or communication, that relationship will normally go by the wayside.

Peter: Going back to your own personal experience—and maybe you can talk about this better than I can because it's your relationship—you mentioned you had all these very wealthy guys who had big bank accounts. But you weren't chasing the money because you had a different value set that you were looking for in a guy.

Could you share one or two of the values you were looking for that helped you find Jim?

Renée: I've been doing a lot of thinking about that recently. Finance, freedom, and health are some of my top values. But one of the top, top values is spirituality, so believing in God was very important (I'm not a religious fanatic, because I'm more spiritual than I am religious). The other top value is family. Would you like me to elaborate a little bit about family?

Peter: Yes. Jim's an old Irishman, so he must have a big family.

Renée: A huge, loving family. In the first or second page of my manifestation letter, I asked for someone over fifty with a family and who's been married once or twice. So I was looking for a guy who's had a lot of experience with women. (If I were a third or fourth wife, I might have been a bit concerned that I was just there as a trophy wife.)

Jim has a wonderful family, and he has a great relationship with his ex-wife. He has a beautiful relationship with his son, Christopher, and he also has a phenomenal relationship with his mother and father. He has great communication with his five brothers and sisters. Even though they don't speak to each other all the time, they're a close-knit family, and you can feel that in their hearts.

We recently had a family reunion. You could definitely feel that their energy was high, and that they were all very loving and caring toward each other.

Peter: But I have to ask you this: Your value was family (we're going to talk shortly about how you determine your values), but priorities sound very important as well. Obviously, spirituality and family were top priorities for you.

Going back to where you were telling me a story about Jim's family, since that was important to you, you must feel like you've become part of his family. You're connected that way now?

Renée: Yes.

Peter: So you were looking for the ideal person to spend the rest of your life with where you could become part of another person's loving family. And you would be part of the family just like your mate was part of the family.

Renée: Yes. But family is more than just great communication and how you nurture and cherish each other. When you have a family that has bonds of love, caring, integrity, and sincerity, then when something happens, the way they react to something—negatively or positively—is directly or indirectly connected to me.

For example, let's say a woman like myself meets a guy who was in a bad relationship with an ex-wife (or wives) and he'd call them names. Then he also had bad relationships with his three or four kids. They're doing poorly in school, they're getting arrested or receiving DUIs, they're on a lot of drugs or getting money from stealing, and things like that. On top of that, he's had bad relationships with his mother and father and his siblings. Most likely, that trait will affect my relationship with him if I choose to be with him. Do you see the distinction?

Peter: I totally understand it.

Renée: However, if the woman likes drama and chaos, and she likes to fix people, then she can go ahead and get involved in that relationship. But then there won't be peace, harmony, bliss, centeredness, or balance. Some women thrive on chaos and being

Cinderella. "Oh, I'll fix them and everything will be fine."

Peter: We actually have someone like that in our family who loves drama and chaos, so I understand what you're talking about. You just laid the groundwork really well for values and beliefs.

Renée: The whole point of this book and me helping people is to share what has helped me: I found peace and happiness, so I'd like to help other people find the love, peace, and bliss I've found. It's become my mission to share my knowledge and experiences to help others have the best relationships they possibly can.

For Jim and me, it's not huggy-bear, kissy-face, or hunky-dory every day. We're married and in a relationship. We have conflict and resolution, but it's how we create safety within that conflict and resolution that ensures we always come together at the end of the day.

If you don't have the tools or the type of personality where you actually listen to each other, then at the end of the day, there's always chaos and you can't come up with a resolution. Stress and chaos create an environment perfect for harboring cancer and other diseases. You live a shorter life.

I want to live a very long life, so I created this atmosphere and environment of love and happiness to be around the right person and his family because his family values come into my life as well. So that was the whole point of knowing yourself and your values before you look for the right person. Do you understand what I'm saying?

Peter: It totally makes sense. The only thing I have to add to that is because you identified your values and beliefs—and you found someone like-minded with the same values and beliefs—even if there's occasionally day-to-day conflict, the connection is never lost. Is that right?

Renée: Correct.

Peter: You always have that connection with that person. You might have an argument here or there, but the connection doesn't go away.

Like you were talking about, if you don't know yourself—know your values and beliefs so you can find that other person who has similar values and beliefs—you can't form that connection and you have no foundation. So if there's conflict, there's no connection that makes you always want to be with that other person. That's what it seems like to me. Is that right?

Renée: That's absolutely correct. We've literally gone through the vow of "thick and thin" patches in our businesses. We've hung in there with each other to support and love each other, and to cry on each other's shoulders. But we always have each other. The "thin" part is when you know that person is going to hang in there with you. Does that make sense?

Peter: It makes total sense. I've had an experience with when it was thin and the person didn't support me. It didn't feel very good.

Renée: You don't want somebody to bail on you when the chips are down so you're left thinking, *I really thought that person was going to be there with me.* It's very important.

Peter: Let's move forward now. So we've got a really good understanding of values, beliefs, and what they are and what yours are.

Can you help us understand how to determine your values and then someone else's true values? Let's start first with tips on how to understand your own values. I believe values are very similar to core desires, which are liberty, legacy, financial freedom, health, autonomy, and knowledge. Are these baseline things that you hold near and dear to you the same kind of thing?

Renée: Yes. You hold these top things close to you. For example, let's say the belief has to do with finance. If I decide as an entrepreneur that I want to make X number of dollars per month—but my belief is there are things on TV I want to watch, I want to go shopping, I want to do this, and I want to do that—there's nothing going toward my business plan. I'm not going to appointments, I'm not returning phone calls, I'm not meeting new clients (or I don't have any clients). I'm just lying on the couch, or I'm out shopping and spending money I don't have on a credit card. That's not being congruent with my values.

The belief is I just want to play and have a good time—so to say my value is to make a certain amount of money is just delusional.

Peter: In this book, you're going to lay out top values for people to choose from (e.g., spirituality, family, finances, health, creativity) to help them identify what their values are. They can look at that list and say, "Yes, that's my value set." I also understand from what you said earlier that they need to prioritize those values.

Renée: I think people should come up with five or six values at the very least. We all live with certain principles on how we live our lives, make our decisions, and which people we surround ourselves with. But innately as humans, we have seven or eight top values. If you're a deep person—you're self-evolved and really know yourself—then you'll know what those top values are. But the beliefs have to match them.

Peter: After you identify your top seven values, I guess you'd then want to look at your life and ask yourself, "Based on my actions, am I living my life with these values correctly or incorrectly?"

Renée: Right. Like spending money. You can think about spending money, but you can't spend money when you don't have any.

Peter: In other words, if you want to find the true love of your life, the person you're going to be with, the first thing you have to work on is getting your values and beliefs into alignment with each other. Right?

Renée: Yes, absolutely first.

Peter: First, before you go find someone?

Renée: Yes. You know how the Law of Attraction works—like attracts like—so the person you're going to attract is who you are. You have to be who you are first before you attract that person.

Peter: Let's say you understand your own values, and you've looked at your beliefs and everything is in alignment—and you have a better understanding of knowing yourself. Then how do you determine someone else's true values?

Renée: You ask him or her probing questions in an interview-type conversation without being obvious that it's an interview. After you've had coffee or juice dates, that's when you journal the questions you've peppered into a conversation, but we'll discuss that in more detail later in this book.

Peter: Let's go back to your example about Jim and your own personal situation. You said family was maybe number two in your values. When you were first starting to get to know Jim, you found out that he had a really big family with five brothers and sisters, which was a plus. But like you said, you probably were digging for a while, maybe asking yourself, "Is this a family that's loving and caring toward each other, or one that's fighting with high drama and anger all the time?" Correct?

Renée: Correct.

Peter: And that kind of got you to, *Wow, this is a really great family.* So I guess the next step was over time you got to meet Jim's family to verify that *Wow, these guys are incredible!*

Renée: Right. You pepper into a conversation questions about the person's relationships and how he relates to his father, mother, brothers, and sisters. You ask him, "When did you get together for Christmas, an anniversary, party, or family reunion? What was that like? Tell me more about that." Or things like that. God gave us two ears and one mouth so we could listen and ask key questions.

Asking key questions—especially on the first and second date—gets it out of the way. And then you get into more depth about who the person is, and what the two of you have in common. So you first get the key questions out of the way. Then you can say, "Yes, I really like this person," or "No, I need to delete him and move on." But you know right away.

Also, if children are one of your top values (I mentioned family, which includes relationships with mothers, fathers, ex-wives, brothers, and sisters), ask the children whether they want to have a family. Maybe they're forty-five or fifty, and they've been married once or twice, but they want to have more children. Is that important to them? Is that important to you? It should be out there.

Or if they're in their thirties and haven't been married before, do they want kids? Some guys want kids—some don't. I tell women all the time, "Don't get pregnant unless it's planned." But if you get pregnant, that's just the way it is. If you're being stupid and not taking precautions, you don't want to be involved with somebody because that's for the rest of your life. You don't want that as an obligation; you want it to be planned as much as you can.

Things happen, but that means you take responsibility for your life. Don't complain. If you have to work three jobs and you're a single mom, take the responsibility. That's it. Step up.

It's the same for a man. If you get someone pregnant, step up. You've got to help support the woman and your child.

Peter: To wrap up this first chapter, "Knowing Yourself," I hope everybody who is reading this book understands why you made this Chapter 1. Because if it were Chapter 4 or 5, after you've gone through a whole bunch of other stuff and found the person—and you're now in a long-term relationship—if you didn't know yourself, then the relationship would not be built on solid ground, so you might have to loop back to square one. So I completely understand why you put "Knowing Yourself" first, followed by knowing how to spot values and beliefs in other people by asking them key questions.

Renée: Yes, but I'd like to add: Don't confuse values and beliefs with hobbies and interests.

Peter: In your mind, what is the distinction between values and beliefs and hobbies and interests?

Renée: Let's say somebody's top value is she needs a lot of relaxation and she wants to stay at home, so "peace" is her value. Her belief is: *To have peace, I stay at home and read* (or knit, crochet, watch TV, hang out with my dog or cat, or watch my fish). That's the distinction.

When you're dating somebody, these are the kinds of questions you want to ask. For instance, I like peace. I like reading books, but I also like going for a run. But some people don't like staying at home; some people always want to be out going to the driving range and playing golf (which, by the way, I like to do also).

You also have to make sure that part of that peace and centeredness the other person may have in his or her life (e.g., the person likes to go skiing or be very active in sports) is always aligned with the questions you ask to make sure you're compatible in that downtime when you want to spend time with your best friend.

If the other person finds reading at home or doing puzzles to be fun, but you find it really boring and you like to be out all the time, there's going to be conflict.

Another value is religion. Let's say if a woman is a devout Christian, but the person she falls in love with is a devout Muslim, that's going to be a huge conflict. Yes, the sex may be good, but it's only going to last a short time because people's religious beliefs are going to be tearing them apart. Or you may not even get together. But that's the part that's really important, especially if both people are really fanatical about their religious beliefs. I want to make sure people understand that.

Peter: That's very good. So I guess the hierarchy is first to know your and your prospective partner's values and beliefs to ensure they are congruent. Then explore your hobbies and interests to see how many of them are similar. Correct?

Renée: Right. Remember we talked about being best friends? If there are too many opposites and things in contrast, like one person likes to stay at home, but the other one likes to go running, or one person is an introvert and doesn't like to socialize, but the other person likes to have parties at home all the time, you're going to have issues.

Imagine that Jim just wants to stay home, be quiet, have the TV on, and watch sports with nobody at home but me, but I like to party and have thirty or forty people over every weekend—that would be a conflict. Does that make sense?

Peter: It makes total sense.

Renée: Jim and I do like to entertain.

Peter: I know you do. Because we're friends, one thing I know about is your hobbies and interests as they relate to cooking and the expression of that hobby. I can tell you guys have a connection and love through food. You love to do that together.

Renée: Oh, yes. We love to cook together. We love to cook for people we love—like we love you and Patricia. Showing how we love you guys is how we cook for you.

The food you see on the plate when we put it on the table comes from love. It's not from a mechanical, cold recipe you follow. You can taste the difference in something at a restaurant when the chef was having a great day. But if he had an argument with his wife, the food won't have any taste or it'll be burned. You can tell whether food was made from love.

Peter: That makes total sense. So let's end this chapter. We now understand the difference between values and beliefs and hobbies and interests. You gave a lot of great examples about how you can really get to know yourself.

Chapter 2 will be about knowing what you really want. Your key question there will be: What is love by design?

Summary

Knowing yourself is imperative before you begin looking for your soulmate. Who you are is not the job you perform or the hobbies and sports you spend you time on. It's much deeper than that.

A value is the characteristic of who you are. It is non-negotiable. Most people have seven to ten values they focus on. Values are the lenses through which we see life and make decisions. They are formed at a very early age and follow us throughout our lives.

Beliefs are also what direct our actions in life, but they are not as concrete as values. A belief is a function of experience, and if an experience changes or the information that contributes to an experience changes, the belief can adjust or change completely.

Hobbies and interests may be influenced by our values and beliefs, but they are not the core of who we are. Many people base their relationships on hobbies and interests more than what they truly believe in. They may get along as a couple at first, but their individual values and beliefs will rule the direction of their relationship and their decision-making so they need to be compatible. So know yourself first.

Homework:

Give yourself the gift of discovering your top seven or eight values. Read the following twenty questions to help you get into the introspective mood. Take a clean sheet of paper, or better yet, get yourself a notebook or journal devoted to the work you are now doing for yourself and a blue-ink pen (make sure it's blue—I'll explain why later)—and answer the questions to the best of your ability. Once you have completed that part (don't forget the bonus question below the twenty questions), write what you think and feel are your top values. Remember, they have to be items that are a must in your life and non-negotiable. Don't worry about the order at first; just get them down on paper. If you have more than seven or eight values, that's okay, but be aware that the top seven or eight values will impact you the most in a long-term relationship.

Once you have your set of top values, put them in order of importance. Take your time on this process. Your values hierarchy is almost as important as the values themselves, so take your time and enjoy the process.

Remember, this is the foundation for everything else you're going to do here on out, so don't rush to get to the fun part of the exercise that outlines what you're looking for because without this foundation, nothing you build will be likely to last or stand strong. In fact, if you didn't complete the rest of this book, you would have more success by just doing this exercise than from anything else you would learn in this book. That's how important it is to know yourself first.

Here are some interesting and introspective questions that might help you find out who you are, what you value, and what your beliefs are:

- ❤ What is your idea of ultimate happiness?

- ❤ What are you most fearful of?

- ❤ What character trait do you most hate about yourself?

- ❤ What trait do you hate most in others?

- ❤ Which person do you most admire who is living or deceased?

- ❤ What is your greatest extravagance?

- ❤ What do you consider the most over-rated virtue?

- ❤ What do you dislike about your appearance?

- ❤ What is the quality you most like in a man or woman?

- ❤ Who or what is the greatest love of your life?

- ❤ Where and when are you happiest?

- ❤ If you could change one thing about yourself, what would it be?

- ❤ What do you consider your greatest achievement?

- ❤ Where would you most like to live?

- ❤ What is your most treasured possession?

- ❤ What do you most value in your friends?

- ❤ What is it that you most dislike?

- ❤ What is your greatest regret?

- ❤ How would you like to die?

❤ What is your motto?

"What I know about myself for sure is _____."

To help you determine what your top seven or eight values may be, review the following list of values and circle the ten values that speak to you. List them on a separate piece of paper. Then put them in hierarchal order of importance from one to ten and keep that for you. Put into your notebook or journal your top seven or eight values.

List of Values

A-D	E-M	O-Z
Abundance	Eagerness	Obedience
Acceptance	Economy	Open-Mindedness
Accomplishment	Ecstasy	Openness
Achievement	Education	Optimism
Acknowledgment	Effectiveness	Order
Activeness	Elegance	Originality
Adaptability	Empathy	Outrageousness
Adoration	Encouragement	Passion
Adventure	Endurance	Peace

A-D	E-M	O-Z
Affection	Energy	Perfection
Affluence	Enjoyment	Perseverance
Aggressiveness	Entertainment	Persistence
Altruism	Enthusiasm	Persuasiveness
Ambition	Excellence	Philanthropy
Appreciation	Excitement	Playfulness
Approachability	Expertise	Pleasure
Assertiveness	Exploration	Power
Attractiveness	Expressiveness	Practicality
Balance	Extravagance	Preparedness
Beauty	Exuberance	Proactivity
Being the Best	Fairness	Professionalism
Bliss	Faith	Prosperity
Boldness	Fame	Realism
Bravery	Family	Reliability

A-D	E-M	O-Z
Brilliance	Fashion	Religiousness
Calmness	Fearlessness	Resilience
Candor	Fierceness	Resourcefulness
Care	Financial Independence	Respect
Carefulness	Fitness	Sacrifice
Certainty	Flexibility	Security
Challenge	Focus	Self-Control
Charity	Fortitude	Selflessness
Chastity	Frankness	Self-Reliance
Cheerfulness	Freedom	Sensitivity
Clarity	Friendliness	Sensuality
Cleanliness	Frugality	Serenity
Clear-Mindedness	Fun	Service
Cleverness	Generosity	Sexuality
Comfort	Giving	Significance

A-D	E-M	O-Z
Commitment	Grace	Sincerity
Compassion	Gratitude	Skillfulness
Connection	Gregariousness	Sophistication
Consistency	Growth	Spirit
Contribution	Happiness	Spirituality
Control	Harmony	Strength
Cooperation	Health	Success
Courage	Helpfulness	Sympathy
Courtesy	Heroism	Synergy
Creativity	Holiness	Teamwork
Credibility	Honesty	Thoroughness
Cunning	Honor	Thrift
Curiosity	Hopefulness	Tidiness
Daring	Hospitality	Timeliness
Decisiveness	Humility	Traditionalism

A-D	E-M	O-Z
Dependability	Humor	Trustworthiness
Determination	Independence	Truth
Devoutness	Integrity	Understanding
Dignity	Intelligence	Unflappability
Diligence	Joy	Uniqueness
Directness	Knowledge	Victory
Discipline	Leadership	Vitality
Discovery	Liberty	Wealth
Dominance	Love	Winning
Duty	Loyalty	Wisdom
Dynamism	Making a Difference	Youthfulness

My Top Values are:

1. _____
   _____

2. _____
   _____

3. _____
   _____

4. _____
   _____

5. _____
   _____

6. _____
   _____

7. _____
   _____

8. _____
   _____

9. _____
   _____

10. _____
    _____

My Top Values in Order of Importance to Me:

1. _____
   _____

2. _____
   _____

3. _____
   _____

4. _____
   _____

5. _____
   _____

6. _____
   _____

7. _____
   _____

8. _____
   _____

9. _____
   _____

10. _____
    _____

CHAPTER 2

Knowing What You Want

"Insanity: doing the same thing over and over
again and expecting different results."

— Albert Einstein

Now that you know who you are and what values and beliefs you live by, you are ready to attract your love at last! In this chapter, we'll discover what Love by Design™ is and how it can benefit you. We'll explore how understanding the reticular activation system (RAS) can help you in your quest to find your love at last. And I'll explain how a manifestation letter can be your most powerful tool for finding your Mr. or Mrs. Right. By using the power of your unconscious, you can attract what you want by only reading about it twice a day. You'll come to understand why you keep attracting the wrong person for you and how to turn it around to attract only what you want. One simple focus can help you identify whether or not you're going in the right direction.

So let's return to our conversation to continue our journey toward manifesting love at last!

Peter: Renée, I've often heard you talk about "love by design," so let's begin there. Will you explain what it means?

Renée: Love by design means taking time to design what your ideal mate looks, sounds, and feels like. Maybe you imagine him or her in your living room or at your kitchen table having a cup of coffee and reading the newspaper. What type of quality time can you envision spending with this person? What does he talk about? What goals does she set for herself? How many showers does he take in a day (don't laugh; that's actually one of my own design points)?

Most people spend more time planning a vacation than planning for their ideal mate. They leave it up to total chance or fate to provide them with Mr. or Mrs. Right. Spending time designing your ideal person is key to finding or manifesting your ideal mate. Even better is not only thinking about him or her, but also writing it down in what I call a manifestation letter or visually representing it on a vision board.

Peter: I know, Renée, that you even get into using specific colors of ink and paper in writing this down. But for now, talk us through the process of creating a manifestation letter.

Renée: The way most people go about meeting their ideal mate is basically the luck of the draw. If you don't write a manifestation letter, you'll attract a lot of people you don't want to have around you. It's kind of like an affirmation letter of whom you want, which excludes what you don't want.

If you've ever written a business plan, you know you write a one-, three-, or five-year projection plan of how you want your business to grow, what the profits are at the end of the year, and how you want to get to those financial goals.

But with a manifestation letter, you want to write down exactly what you want—not what you don't want, because then you will attract what you don't want. Peter, would you like me to give you an example?

Peter: Sure. Go ahead.

Renée: For instance, let's say you would like to attract a man over fifty. Men over fifty most likely have been married once or twice. Let's say you're a woman in your late thirties or forties. You love kids, but you don't like kids under ten years old because dating and having young children is harder on the family. Whereas children who are fifteen or older would be ideal because they're more mature and can handle their parents' separation, and they can also handle their now single parent's newfound love.

So in order to attract children over fifteen, you don't want to write "I don't like little kids" or "I don't want young kids" in your manifestation letter. Your letter has to focus only on what you do want in your life. This is key to attracting the person you want. Your mind and the Universe (you can use the word God, Creator, Mother Earth, or anything that makes you feel more comfortable—I use Universe) does not understand the idea of negatives. So rather than say, "I don't want a man who is bald," you'd say, "I want a man with a full head of hair."

The next step is to write your description in the present tense, so using the full head of hair example, I would write, "My man, or my ideal mate, has a full head of hair." Writing in the present tense is an important part of writing your manifestation letter. By stating it in the present tense, you are telling the universe that you are ready for it now instead of writing "I want…" which perpetually puts it in the future just outside your grasp.

Peter: So this manifestation letter has your entire list of wants (for lack of a better word). Your example may be tied to your value of wanting a family. However, do you go into every little characteristic in this letter (e.g., what he/she looks like; the color of his/her hair, eyes, etc.)? How specific do you get?

Renée: I get very specific, and the letter you write is for your eyes only, so don't hold back in writing every little detail that's important to you. You want to write down as much as possible to describe not just the tree in the forest, but also every leaf and branch on the tree. You want to go into minute detail, starting with the person's values and beliefs because, as we discovered in Chapter 1: Knowing Yourself, they are the foundation for a great relationship.

From my experiences, with respect to the nine gentlemen to whom I was previously engaged, it may have looked like everything was ideal on the outside—each man was good looking, had a great character, a sense of humor, a good source of income, and I liked his financial blueprint for how he viewed money in general, but what I was missing was that deeper, inner connection through values and beliefs. I did what most people do who take the time to think about what they are looking for and focus on the external; I looked at what we call the "what looks good on paper" attributes. I learned the hard way that focusing only on those attributes will never get you what you truly yearn for in a loving, complete relationship.

What looks good on paper is for the short term. When you go into it deeper and you see he's got a terrible relationship with his ex-wife and/or his mother and father, he doesn't get along with his siblings, and he has no friends, only then do you see those warning signs that something is off. By then, it could be too late because you're already stuck in the wrong relationship and unhappy, or you're headed for a breakup.

The reason I say this is because if you're like me and you want to create peace, harmony, and a stress-free life, you need to start with writing down your ideal mate's values and beliefs first. From this manifestation letter, you attract a loving and kind person who has a good set of values with his family and friends; that is a good indicator that it will also be how he treats you and your family because you marry his entire family and he marries your entire family.

It's not that everybody has to be huggy-bear, kissy-face all of the time. But just in general, as a kind of warning to be aware of, if someone has three or four kids and he and the kids argue a lot, they don't see each other on holidays, or they never speak to each other because of friction, chaos, or drama—you'll get the same thing later in your relationship with that person.

Now you can see why this second step in the process is so important and why you need to take the time to outline clearly the person of your dreams. Don't do what most people do, which is to settle. Do not settle for that person who may not be whom you want to be with and then try to fix him or her. Life is too short to try to fix everybody. You can care for the person and hope he or she gets help. But it's that person's responsibility to get help. Therefore, if you allow people to be, they'll get fixed on their own. Imagine how much better off you would be if the time you spent trying to fix someone to be the person of your dreams, you instead spent toward writing down at the beginning the complete person you deserve.

Peter: Let's talk about that a little bit, and then we'll get into some of these key areas of designing your optimal partner. I can only speak from a guy's perspective, but I've noticed that a lot of women will go into a relationship trying to fix a man. As a "relationship master," why do you think that's not a good idea?

Renée: It's not a good idea because many people aren't trained therapists or coaches. If I'm going into a relationship, I'd rather have that person be who he is authentically. I wouldn't go into a relationship if the person were not resonating with me, or we weren't on the same vibration with regard to values and beliefs.

You don't want to go into a relationship trying to fix someone; you just want to enjoy his or her company and live your life. God didn't put us on Earth to fix each other. We're put together to learn from each other, and to be journey partners as we move through life together. We're not the Island of the Misfit Toys, and we're not here to fix broken toys.

Peter: That's so true.

Renée: And it's much nicer. You live a more fulfilling life not being in the fix-it mode. You have a fulfilling life learning and growing with each other.

Yes, there are ups and downs if you've been married ten, twenty, or thirty years. But learning from and growing with each other is the key. You take the vow of "for better or for worse, for richer, for poorer, in sickness and in health" because you want to be with that person through thick and thin, and ride up and down on the waves together. You're not trying to criticize, critique, or fix—you just want to move forward holding hands.

Peter: As long as we're talking about what you want and what you don't want, the other thing I've noticed is that people get into relationships because they're lonely. Can you speak to that a little as well?

Renée: Absolutely. There's a credo I live by: "I'd rather be alone and happy than married and miserable." I shared this statement in Chapter 1, but it's worth repeating.

When I was dating my husband, Jim, we talked a lot over the phone for the first few months of the relationship. We had what you call a long distance relationship. I lived in Southern California and he lived in Silicon Valley, California. Before I even saw his photo (he wasn't online on Match.com, so he only got to see my photo), we talked a lot. During our conversations and when we finally saw each other in person, he told me he'd said to himself, "I'd rather be alone than with somebody I need to fill a void with." I had thought the same thing: I'd rather be alone and happy by myself because I like myself, than being married and miserable with somebody.

What was remarkable was that we both made this statement separately on the same day! It was the day before Jim found me on Match.com, the day he first reached out to me. We believe that statement that we both made, independent of each other, was a way we were able to communicate to the universe that we were ready to meet. We made the declaration that we were okay by ourselves and didn't need another person to complete us.

You aren't with somebody just to make you feel whole. People should feel whole within themselves because all the other person does when you meet him or her is give you companionship and love. That person shouldn't have to fill a void in your heart.

My opinion is that it's better to go through life with someone you connect with completely. It's best to be two complete human beings who, when they come together, become more than the sum of their parts. God made us to grow together, whether it's with a man or a woman—whatever your preference.

Peter: In knowing yourself and knowing what you want in a relationship, if a person is feeling lonely, what should he or she be working on first before entering into a relationship? Or is it okay to start looking for a relationship if you're feeling lonely?

Renée: You need to ask yourself why you're feeling empty, so work on yourself first to become fulfilled. Get a coach or enter a personal development program. But definitely get on track and become aware of what your strong suits are as well as what you're lacking. Work on yourself so that when you find that person, you'll be truly authentic to who you are. It's okay to yearn for companionship as a result of the work you've done on yourself. But you want to be sure that you get into a complete, loving relationship for the right reasons, like wanting to share a life with someone special.

Now, there's nothing wrong with being alone. But being alone and feeling lonely are two different things.

Peter: The message I'm hearing you say loud and clear is if you go down that pathway while you're lonely, it may be a short-term gain for a long-term sacrifice. But you're really speaking to the long-term gain of having a partner for the rest of your life. So if you're going to fix anybody, fix yourself instead of someone else.

I like your idea of a personal coach and getting some things taken care of so you feel okay with yourself and with being alone. Then you can move forward to a long-term gain and a lifetime relationship with someone.

Renée: Exactly. One of the things my dad always said when I was seven or eight years old was that "Just like a bus, there will always be another guy around the corner every five minutes. So don't worry about it."

Peter: That's a good way to put it.

Renée: Of course, for me, it would have been a boy at the time, or a man now (well, not now because I'm married). It isn't like you're going to run out of people. For instance, when I was online, 2,874 people emailed me. There are tons of people, so it's just attracting that right person. I only wanted five or six people to select from, and then I finally chose one. When you come from a place of being lonely, you come from a place of scarcity. When you think that all the good guys or gals are taken, well, it becomes true because you, through your statement, have manifested that fact. So accept a new fact: Limitless possibilities of people are available to you, so you might as well take the time to outline specifically what Mr. or Mrs. Right is to you!

Peter: Going back to key areas and designing your optimal partner, you had touched a little bit on writing out the details. And you mentioned something about blue ink and white paper. Why is that important?

Renée: Blue ink on white paper resonates with your ability to manifest or create for yourself. I think it has a lot to do with the reticular activation system or RAS that triggers a specific focus reaction in your brain. In my experience, I've found that blue versus black or red ink on white paper has always resonated better with me and also with the Universe. Purple is my favorite color, but blue ink is absolutely the best for manifesting.

Peter: We'll talk a bit about the neuroscience aspect a little later in the chapter. But for now, what other key areas should people write down to manifest what they want in a partner?

Renée: Not just values and beliefs, but also what you want the person's hobbies and interests to be to make sure you have some sort of compatibility.

I've found that the more you have in common with the person, the more fun it can be. However, there are ways to enjoy each other even if your interests are different. For instance, you meet a guy who likes playing golf, but you don't like playing golf. You can always ride in the cart and watch him on the driving range and still spend quality time together. Or if you both like reading books in your living room—but you're on one couch and he's on another—

you're still spending quality quiet time together. So interests and hobbies are really important.

But you can go to the extreme. If you constantly like to entertain and have people over, but the person you're involved with is more of an introvert (there's nothing wrong with that), there will be conflict, especially if you consistently want to have twenty or thirty people to your home for an elaborate, gourmet dinner.

Another example is religion versus spirituality. If one person is an open-minded Christian and more spiritual than tied down to specific religious practices, and the other person is an extreme Muslim, the relationship isn't going to work because of their conflicting beliefs. It just isn't going to happen. You may be physically attracted to each other, but it won't work for a long-term relationship.

You also marry the person's family, so if both families are very religious from two very different faiths, there will be conflict, but you don't want that kind of conflict and chaos in your life.

Peter: The message here is to be as detailed and thorough as you need to be when writing your manifestation letter. How long was yours?

Renée: I think it was about fifty-two pages.

Peter: Wow! So it was like an entire book.

Renée: It was almost like a book. It was on a white, legal-sized pad, so it was longer. I kept it by my bed and read it twice a day.

Peter: All fifty-two pages?

Renée: All fifty-two pages because it was really important for me to find the right person since I had been engaged nine times. I kept wondering what I was doing to attract all these wonderful people whom, a couple of months or a few weeks before the wedding, I had to tell "This isn't going to work." Something triggered itself inside me that made me think the person wasn't going to be around for my entire life. So I was committed to the process of being very clear about what was important to me. I would continually ask, "What characteristics in my ideal mate would contribute to a complete loving life together?"

So did fifty-two pages really seem like a lot? Not for the result I was searching for. You should look at this manifestation letter as a living entity in the sense that it is continually evolving and becoming more specific and detailed. The process of writing my manifestation letter kept me in conversation with God about what I was looking for in a partner. I didn't sit down and write fifty-two pages all at once. I kept adding to my letter on a daily basis. Like I mentioned already, I would read it twice a day, just before I would close my eyes and go to sleep and again when I would wake in the morning. It would be at those times that I might add or adjust details to my description of the love of my life.

Peter: It sounds like if you did that amount of work, I'd probably want to marry Jim.

Renée: He's a good guy, but he doesn't swing that way.

Peter: A good point to make here is that you hadn't gotten to this level of detail about knowing what you wanted in your previous nine engagements, which is why you had issues with them.

Renée: Yes. They were wonderful men—all multimillionaires, which on paper looks phenomenal. But when it came to the reality, I thought, *Do I want to be with this person and sleep with him every single night for the rest of my life? Do I really want this?* I answered, "No, it won't work."

I'm not keen on divorce. I'm very committed and loyal, so I knew whomever I gave my heart to would have to be someone absolutely fantastic on a deeper level than just on the surface and in terms of his bank account.

Peter: We talked about that—that a good relationship has that true connection, and not just surface desires and common hobbies and interests.

What we've been talking about in these first two chapters is finding that person you can have that connection with. Right?

Renée: Correct.

Peter: I've heard a lot of men and women say, "It doesn't really matter, just as long as he or she loves me." Or "It's like for better or worse. I'll take all the lumps just as long as he or she loves me." How do you respond to that?

Renée: It takes more than that, especially if your values and beliefs are incongruent. Love is love, but it does wear out. So are you attracted to that person? Can you live with him or her, or do you want to be distant and be like roommates? Or do you want to have a loving relationship physically and emotionally?

If it's incongruent, and it's just one person loving the other person, it's not really fulfilling, and then on your deathbed, you're going to die kind of detached.

Peter: A quote I love is from Thoreau. In essence, he said that the majority of people lead lives of quiet desperation, which I think is sad, not just in terms of fulfilling your dreams but in finding that perfect partner to be with here on Earth. What you're kind of warning people about here is not to give in to living that life of quiet desperation.

Renée: Exactly. Peter, life is really short. We're all living in a little dash of time from the time we're born until the time we die. You even see it on people's gravestones. I just saw my father's gravestone the other day at the cemetery. He was a great man who contributed a lot to me, his family, his friends, and his community. He made a great impact on this Earth, and I want to do the same.

There are many things you can do to fill in that little dash. You want to leave a legacy of what you've accomplished in terms of your businesses, the hearts of your family and friends you've touched with your love, and the relationship you created with the love of your life.

Peter: That's probably the deepest connection you can have. I totally understand what you're saying.

Let's go back to the ideas you touched on earlier in the chapter about the reticular activation system and your manifestation letter. How does the brain science of the reticular activator system (RAS) apply to the power of attraction? What's a good example that can help people understand how powerful it really is?

Renée: It's powerful in that the Law of Attraction is not about repeating what you've done in the past. You need to become aware of your past habits and behaviors that didn't serve you and then create a new set by correcting them.

When you break up a relationship like a marriage or even a relationship with a casual boyfriend or girlfriend, take time to think about what you did to attract that relationship in the first place. Let's say it was a physically or mentally abusive relationship. I tell people, "Don't get involved with another relationship until you work on yourself; otherwise, your RAS and the Law of Attraction will attract the same wrong person over and over. It'll become a habit because you'll subconsciously be comfortable attracting wrong people, but consciously, you'll be unaware of it." I call finding the same wrong person over and over and then going through a repeated heartbreak being "comfortable sitting in your poop." As strange as that may sound, we all get something out of every experience. Even if we look at that experience—in this case, constantly attracting the wrong person—as a negative experience, we still get something that we need or want from it—even if it's only short term. And after all, when we do it enough, it becomes very familiar to our unconscious self, and there is a certain level of comfort with familiarity.

Now, the more you work on your manifestation letter, the more you are focused on what you really want in a partner. I look at the RAS as a sorting machine in your brain. You put the search parameters on paper—blue ink to white paper. You read them twice a day at times when you are most receptive to suggestion (your suggestions). You then let the RAS do the sorting unconsciously. Jim and I have talked about this phenomenon in relation to how we met. We ran in different circles, so meeting casually would not have been possible. He worked in corporate America doing leadership trainings and team-building programs; I was an entrepreneur, so I wouldn't be attending a corporate training program. Jim wasn't even a member of Match.com when he found me on it. He just happened to go on it to check out his (girl) friend's profile to make her profile more "guy friendly," and my profile happened to be located just above his friend's profile. It seemed the more I focused on what or who I wanted and less on how I would find him, the closer and closer our RAS sorting machine brought us. Peter, you probably have some scientific data to back up what I experienced in finding the love of my life.

Peter: I like the way you talk about that. Yes, as you know, I've done a lot of work in brain research, and I'll share some new research done by the University of Washington just this past year.

The reticular activation system in your brain is kind of like a filter. In fact, it sits at the base of your brain, which, through the five senses (sight, sound, smell, taste, and touch), takes in about 11 million bits per second. We only process about twenty bits per second in the thinking part of our brain, so all that stuff is constantly going on.

A good example is if you ever bought a car, and then, all of a sudden, you start seeing the same make and model everywhere on the road.

Renée: Yes. After Jim and I visited a Tesla dealership, we started to see Tesla cars on the road where previous to that visit, we had noticed only a very few. What was even more amazing was that we were seeing the Tesla cars with the same exterior color as Jim imagined his car would have.

Peter: That's the reticular activation system in action. As it relates to relationships and what you're talking about, writing a manifestation letter opens the gates to the filter much wider. Your reality has shifted and changed, and you're allowing the type of person you're defining to come into your life because the filter is now turned off. You've altered your reality.

Like I said, this has been proven by the University of Washington. Some of the researchers in neuroscience there did a very interesting study with a sender and a receiver (which shows how powerful your brain is in relation to the relationship aspect you're talking about).

They hooked up two people who were a half mile apart in two different buildings to EEG swimming caps. The sender was moving the controls of a video game. The researchers were able to take the sender's brain signal and upload it to the Internet, then download it to the receiver, who was using a magnetic cap. They proved the sender could control the receiver's hands and the game movement through their brains.

We're now getting into all new territory in neuroscience. So taking this back to what you're saying about relationships, because you clearly define your perfect partner in a manifestation letter, you're sending out brain signal waves to the receiver who's the ideal mate you're looking for.

This is the science of manifestation—not the woo-woo power of attraction. This stuff actually works, and we're now proving that you can speak brain-to-brain without any physical communication at all.

I think knowing what you want is very powerful, so you have to follow the process. You wrote a fifty-two-page manifestation letter writing down everything little you wanted because only then did you open the reticular activation system.

Renée: Exactly. Like I said, you're in the forest not looking at all the leaves and the branches. But it's literally the minutia, the tiniest little details. You could say, "He's everything," but it's in the details and you could miss one little thing.

Peter: Like why does he pick his nose? I just don't like that.

Renée: Or why does he squeeze the middle of a tube of toothpaste or not put the cap back on? Or why doesn't he put the toilet seat down? It's the little things that irritate you, especially if you're a woman over thirty-five or forty and haven't been married before. (There's nothing wrong with being unmarried for that long because many women are powerful and entrepreneurial these days.)

I happen to be more of a chameleon. I have certain guidelines, but I'm very flexible and adjustable in my lifestyle.

Both men and women get set in their ways. Everyone creates rules, and sometimes those rules become harder and faster as the person gets older and is living on his or her own. Then when the person merges with another person's lifestyle, it can be challenging. So all of this minutia that you can think of has to be written down, which

I didn't do with the other men I was engaged to.

Peter: That's very important. I think we also have to discuss how often people should be reading their manifestation letters to remind them of whom they're designing for themselves.

Renée: They should be reading their manifestation letters at least twice a day: In the morning when they wake up, and also right before they go to bed. Like I said earlier, this manifestation letter is for your eyes only, so it's not to be shared.

If you happen to date online, it's also a guideline for your profile (we will discuss that later). You can use those little details you've written down and compact them into your profile so you get exactly what you want.

Peter: Renée, your manifestation letter was fifty-two pages. But could you take the major points and put them on notecards so you have them with you to look throughout the day? Or should you just read the entire letter?

Renée: You can have notecards with phrases and certain things you want written on them to review whenever you have free time because you never know when or where you're going to meet that person.

You could be online and hoping that when you get home, you'll get a few emails or hits on your profile. But you could also be at the drugstore or grocery store and meet the love of your life in the parking lot because you put it out to the Universe.

Peter: We're now at a point in understanding the brain and neuroscience where what was previously described as the Law of Attraction—and thought by some to be like woo-woo crystal New Age magic—is now scientific fact. In the example I just gave of two people a half-mile away from each other in two different buildings, there was brain control going on with their hands.

So what you're doing is very powerful because you're kind of like an antenna and a beacon. You're communicating your manifestation of what you want, and the right person who meets your criteria is picking up that signal. Now neuroscience studies are showing how that actually happens with the brain, so this is all very good stuff.

Renée, thanks for covering "Knowing What You Want." I really appreciated your information. I encourage our readers now to read the summary and do the exercises and then we'll be ready to move into Chapter 3: Attracting Mr. or Mrs. Right.

Summary:

Knowing what you want is an extension of knowing who you are. Life with your soulmate would be very challenging if you didn't have your core values and beliefs in alignment.

By becoming very clear about what you want in a lifemate and writing it down on white paper with blue ink, it becomes more real to you. Writing it down on paper is called the manifestation letter because that's exactly what you are going to do with this information—manifest the person of your dreams.

Once you are clear and complete with your manifestation letter, you need to read it at least twice a day—once upon rising and once before going to sleep. These are the best times to engage the RAS in your brain. Basically, the RAS creates a filter that helps you identify your love at last when you find him or her. The RAS also sends off a signature vibration and frequency that matches what you are searching for, thus attracting that person to you.

Action Steps: Manifestation Letter

In a new notebook or journal, or in the lines below, begin writing in blue ink your manifestation letter. To get started, use your list and information from Chapter 1: Knowing Yourself as a guideline to get things rolling. Focus first on your ideal mate's values and beliefs; then organize the rest of the manifestation letter in any way you'd like. Remember to write in the present tense as if it has already happened. If you're not one to sit down and write, make it fun while writing. Play your favorite music in the background or start with the easy stuff first, like what kinds of vacations you'd both like to be experiencing, which places you'd like to see, which concerts you'd like to hear. Remember to include in your descriptions and details as much sensory information as possible like what you see, hear, feel, smell, and taste. This is the most important part of the attracting process after "Knowing Yourself." So take your time and enjoy the process. Does this seem like a lot of work? Yes, it is! But I promise you that if you follow the steps exactly as I have outlined them for you, your rewards will outweigh your efforts ten-fold! So be patient; let the power of RAS and your manifestation letter do the heavy lifting. I've included some questions below to stimulate your creative self in this process of Love by Design™. Enjoy!

Bonus Step: "End of the Movie"

(This is for all of those "go-getters" out there committed to finding their Mr. or Mrs. Right quickly.)

Create an "end of the movie" scenario about you and the love of your life. This is a slice of life from the life you've created, starring you and your ideal mate. You can write this short story on note cards that you carry around with you and read during breaks at the office, during commercials on TV, or while waiting for a call. So put down your iPad or cell phone, stop playing Angry Birds, and enjoy a piece of life. Remember, write everything in the present tense, like "my sweetheart and I *are...*" not "my sweetheart and I *will...*." Include in your scenario the following details:

It's Sunday morning and you and your ideal mate are having a leisurely breakfast together. Describe your experience. What aromas do you smell? What do you see? What sounds in the background do you hear? What flavors do you taste? What looks do you get from your lover? What words does he/she say? Remember, you are the star, director, and audience of your "end of the movie" story.

_____

_____

_____

_____

_____

_____

_____

_____

_____

_____

_____

_____

_____

_____

Love by Design™ Questions to Help Fuel Your Creativity in Writing Your Manifestation Letter:

What specific values do you cherish that also need to be in your ideal mate's top seven or eight values?

_____

_____

_____

_____

_____

_____

_____

_____

_____

_____

_____

_____

What specific beliefs of yours need to be compatible with your ideal mate's beliefs?

_____

_____

_____

_____

_____

_____

_____

_____

_____

_____

_____

Describe what your Mr. or Mrs. Right looks like, sounds like, smells like, and feels like:

_____

_____

_____

_____

_____

_____

_____

_____

_____

_____

_____

_____

What activities or hobbies do you like to do together? What are you okay doing apart?

_____

_____

_____

_____

_____

_____

_____

_____

_____

_____

_____

_____

How many showers does your partner need to take as a minimum standard?

_____

Does he/she have kids? How old do the kids have to be? Is there a cut-off age, like no babies, but teens are fine?

_____
_____
_____
_____
_____
_____

Is he/she clean-shaven or does he/she sport facial hair (both men and women!)?

_____

Is your partner physically active? Does he/she play a sport? Are you okay if your partner spends time with that sport?

_____
_____
_____
_____
_____
_____
_____

Is he/she an extrovert or introvert?

_____

Is she/she a dress-up sophisticated type, dress-down casual type, or an appropriate-to-the-occasion kind of person?

_____

Does he/she travel for work? Does he/she work from home?

_____
_____
_____
_____
_____
_____
_____

Is your future partner financially secure? Is money important to him/her?

_____
_____
_____
_____
_____
_____
_____

Does he/she own or rent a home?

_____

Does he/she like to travel?

_____

Is he/she open to personal transformation and development?

_____
_____
_____
_____
_____
_____

Is your future partner religious? Does he/she have to be a specific religion? Is he/she more spiritual with no ties to a church? Does he/she believe in God?

_____
_____
_____
_____
_____
_____
_____
_____
_____

Does your future partner care for pets? What kinds of pets?

_____

_____

_____

_____

_____

_____

Does he/she get along with his/her parents, siblings, and extended family?

_____

_____

_____

_____

_____

_____

Does he/she have close lifelong friends? Activity friends? Work friends?

_____

_____

_____

_____

_____

_____

_____

_____

_____

_____

Does he/she like to dine out? Dine in? Both? Does he/she cook? Clean up? Both?

_____

_____

_____

_____

_____

_____

_____

What kinds of movies does your future partner like? Books? Periodicals? Blogs?

_____

_____

_____

_____

_____

_____

_____

Is he/she active in social media? Does he/she Facebook or tweet?

_____

_____

_____

_____

_____

_____

_____

Is he/she a "joiner," meaning very social or inclusive? Does he/she belong to clubs, the chamber of commerce, networking groups, etc.?

_____

_____

_____

_____

_____

_____

_____

Is he/she a mountain person, a desert person, a city person, or a coastal person?

_____

_____

_____

_____

_____

_____

_____

What is his/her political affiliation? Does your future partner view him- or herself as more liberal, conservative, or moderate?

_____

_____

_____

_____

_____

_____

_____

Does he/she smoke cigarettes? Cigars? Pipes? E-cigarettes?

_____
_____
_____
_____
_____
_____
_____

Does he/she meditate, chant, or pray?

_____
_____
_____
_____
_____
_____
_____

Does he/she enjoy artificially-induced altered states (does he/she like to get high!)? How often and for how long?

_____
_____
_____
_____
_____
_____
_____

Make a list of common dating questions like "Does your ideal mate smoke?" and list them in a column. You can use some of the questions that you just read or add the questions that are important to you. Add three more columns titled: Must, Maybe, and Never. Put a check in the column that best answers your questions. So, for instance, to answer this question about smoking, if you don't care either way whether he or she smokes, check "Maybe." If you checked "Never," then this is what we call a deal breaker and no matter how perfect that person seems to be in other areas, this is the deal breaker and you have to move on. Remember, this is your life. Don't give in to the short-term thrill of finding a partial love of your life. Go all the way to get the person you deserve by sticking to the long-term plan of finding your love at last!

For your complimentary pdf copy of this Love by Design™ form, visit this url http://www.luvatlast.com/luvaluation-tools.htm or scan the following QR code:

Characteristic	Must	Maybe	Never

CHAPTER 3

Attracting Mr. or Mrs. Right

"The Wrong person won't think you're WORTH their love, loyalty or respect. So they'll offer you something less. DON'T ACCEPT IT. Know your worth and move on."

— Sonya Parker

"It sounds like a cliché, but I also learnt that you're not going to fall for the right person until you really love yourself and feel good about how you are."

— Emma Watson

Do you get frustrated because no matter what you do, you keep attracting what I like to call Mr. or Mrs. Wrong? Learn why you keep repeating unwanted old patterns that seem to pull you toward the wrong person every time. Understand that everything you do is determined by your own values and beliefs, so there is hope for you. Learn the three-step process to interrupting your unwanted repeating patterns and keep yourself on track for finding your Mr. or Mrs. Right and your love at last.

So let's dive into this chapter and find out how not to attract Mr. or Mrs. Wrong again!

Peter: All right, Renée. I know this topic of "Attracting Mr. or Mrs. Right" is probably near and dear to your heart since you went through nine engagements that didn't work out, so you got pretty good at finding Mr. Wrong.

Renée: I wouldn't call any of them Mr. Wrong because they were all great guys and multimillionnaires to boot. I would have to call them Mr. Next! However, the mafia hitman I once dated was Mr. Wrong big time. (I won't do that again.)

But you've got to learn from your mistakes. If people don't learn from their mistakes and are comfortable sitting in their poop, they'll keep repeating their history and finding Mr. Wrong.

Peter: A big question people ask is, "Why do I attract the wrong person over and over?" What goes on there?

Renée: Unconsciously, they're comfortable with attracting that same kind of person. So I tell people if you're in a bad relationship, and you break up or the person leaves you, take a break from relationships to assess yourself. As I mentioned in Chapter 2, I tell people, "Don't get involved with another relationship until you work on yourself; otherwise, your RAS and the Law of Attraction will attract the same wrong person over and over. It'll become a habit that you'll unconsciously be comfortable attracting, but consciously, you'll be unaware of it." I call finding the same wrong person over and over and then going through a repeated heart-break as being comfortable sitting in your poop. As strange as that may sound, we all get something out of every experience. Even if we look at that experience, in this case, constantly attracting the wrong person, as a negative experience, we still get something that we need or want from that experience. And after all, when we do it enough, it becomes very familiar to our unconscious self, and there is a certain level of comfort with familiarity.

Let me illustrate what I mean when I say you get something out of every experience even if it's a negative one. This will explain why people who are abused may keep experiencing this unwanted abuse. And please, don't be confused by what and how I'm going to explain this thought pattern to you that an abused person is wanting to be abused. What I am about to explain is how an un-conscious thought pattern that puts an abused person in a com-promising situation will unconsciously give that person something he or she needs or wants.

As strange as it seems, a negative occurrence can supply us with a need without us knowing it. This is why a person who has been physically or verbally abused by a spouse will continually stay with the abusing person. For example, she may know consciously that her spouse is abusing her and that she should not accept this be-havior or that she needs to leave this situation. We've all heard the stories about abused spouses forgiving the abuser and continually going back to him or her regardless of the continual danger. But on an unconscious level, the abused person may be receiving emo-tional attention that she wants or even loves from these attacks that fulfills a deeper need. She may have been abused as a child by her parent, and at a very young and impressionable age, she begins to associate abuse with love, and if this situation is not dealt with, it will continually manifest itself within future close relationships.

Just to reiterate, the abused person does not consciously want this abuse in his or her life, but the person stays because of the familiar feeling experienced during an early impressionable age. That is why I use the expression that you can become comfortable in your own poop because you've found an unconscious meaning and reason why it's good for you!

Get some help like at an emotional bootcamp to kick your butt and jiggle your cage a little bit so you will look at and learn to value yourself; tell yourself that you're worthy of much more than that. In most cases, you need to do something outrageous and out of character to break your unwanted state and replace it with a much more empowered state of awareness. However, our upcoming three-step process should help most people get beyond their challenges of being attracted to the wrong people and put them on the right path to finding Mr. or Mrs. Right!

Peter: So you're saying you've got to step back and reassess what happened and what caused you to pick that person?

Renée: Right. What caused you to pick that person as well as what attracted him or her to you in the first place.

Peter: You talked about stepping back. But can you become a little more specific about what a person needs to do as far as a reassessment? You mentioned the boot camp, but what are some specific things people can do to reassess what they're really looking for and not to attract Mr. or Mrs. Wrong again?

Renée: As I said in the previous chapter about writing your manifestation letter, if you focus more on what you want and less on what you don't want, it will be a big step. If you're used to attracting Mr. or Mrs. Wrong, you will also need a support team or system to help save you from yourself. I tell my clients that if you continue to do what you've done before (in attracting Mr. or Mrs. Wrong), you'll continue to get what you've gotten. So take a bit longer to make a decision. Reassess who is right for you by going back to your own values and beliefs. Does this new person match with you in the areas that keep you safe in a relationship? If you need to, during your reassessment time, use close friends to support your decision. Introduce them to this process and share with them what you're trying to accomplish in your goal to find love at last. If they are any types of friends at all, they will help you. In fact, they were probably the ones who constantly helped you pick up the pieces of your life when you got involved with Mr. or Mrs. Wrong in the past, so they will be more than willing to assist you in a positive process.

The manifestation letter in this instance is key to attracting the right person and putting you on the right path. Peter, is it okay if I quickly go through what to write?

Peter: Sure. Let's get specific.

Renée: "Specific" means how important certain things are in your life. Let's say your top values are family, health, financial security, and religion or spirituality. Another one is finding someone who is intelligent (somebody you can be friends with and communicate with for a while).

Let's first address the value of family. For example, you're close to your parents, you see your brothers and sisters every weekend, and you go to church every Sunday.

However, as you know, everybody is somewhat dysfunctional. Maybe the person you're falling in love with is a loner and doesn't have very many friends. He has bad relationships with his parents (especially his mother), or there's a lot of drama with his grown children. He hates to go to church, he's shy or anxious, and he doesn't like to socialize with people.

It's going to be a huge challenge if he's smothering you and wants to keep you to himself. No matter how much in love you are (maybe you've already slept with him), you have to take a step back and ask from a neutral third person point of view, "Is this person right for me?"

Peter: I guess part of what you're saying is to step back and look at yourself. But going back to your manifestation letter, you need to know what you want—not necessarily what you don't want. Right?

Peter: Correct. Women in general have a tendency to say, "I can change him. He can be the man of my dreams. He can be my Mr. Right if only he does this and this, so I'll wait for him to change."

I always tell everyone to allow people to be who they are and be authentic because that's who you're going to be with for years and years. You can't be with someone by hoping and wishing. Plus, you shouldn't have to work so hard at a relationship; it should be somewhat effortless.

There's always a bit of work in a relationship. It's like pulling weeds out of a beautiful garden every once in a while. But it shouldn't be where you're raking an entire garden that's full of weeds.

If the entire garden is full of overgrown trees and weeds, and you're trying to change it into a beautiful lawn full of flowers and lush greenery, it's not going to happen because there are too many challenges. You have to have flourishing flowers and live plants in order to enjoy your garden.

Life is too short to be an emotional nursemaid to that person, which is why knowing what you want is so crucial to helping you find the love of your life, Mr. Right, or Mr. Happily-Ever-After.

Peter: This gets back to what you were talking about, where if you understand what you're looking for—and your values and beliefs are in alignment—that's where the connection occurs, which is a lot more powerful than just having hobbies and interests with that person. Correct?

Renée: Yes. It goes much deeper. As I mentioned earlier, hobbies and interests will link all that together, but that's at a secondary level. However, values and beliefs go to the core of the person. It doesn't mean that if you're a woman, you have to be interested in football and baseball like the man you're dating.

Peter: Oh, yes you do! (I'm just kidding....)

Renée: I'm often sitting in the family room with Jim while he's watching football or basketball. I'll have a light on, and I'm doing needlepoint or I'm on the computer. But at least we're together. I'm seldom on the phone because I want to give conscious time to him, and he gives that to me.

Peter: And you can watch cooking shows together because that's something you have in common.

Renée: We don't watch too many cooking shows because we're creating our own cooking shows.

Peter: There you go! You're in the kitchen doing it instead of watching it.

Renée: Lots of things are "cooking" in the kitchen.

Peter: We won't go into what else goes on in the kitchen.

Renée: That's another spicy book altogether. (Get it?) That's in my other book, *Garlic to Garter Belts*.

Peter: That actually might be a good book. In Chapter 2, we talked about the science of the reticular activation system (RAS) and the power of attraction. We talked about the RAS as the filtering mechanism in the example of when you a buy car, and all of a sudden you see it everywhere on the road. But how does the RAS apply to relationships as far as opening that new reality to find Mr. or Mrs. Right?

Renée: Like I said earlier, when you write your forty- to fifty-page manifestation letter, what you want will appear. Everything you put on those pages (which are for your eyes only) literally can come to fruition.

Peter: A lot of people who are reading this are probably thinking, I've heard about *The Secret* and all this Law of Attraction foo-foo woo-woo nonsense. But if you believe in that, how does that actually happen?

You told your own story. But maybe you could tell a couple of stories about how people you've worked with went through this process and it actually worked for them.

Renée: I'm going to use an example for people who are non-believers or aren't into the foo-foo woo-woo. I'm going to speak to the left-brain person who's more logical, analytical, or technical.

Some people are entrepreneurs while some aren't since they work for other companies. Successful businesses or entrepreneurs always have a business plan in place. To manifest the relationship I have now, I created a "business plan," which is what these pages of the manifestation letter are. If you write what you specifically want, it will come.

A timeline can also be good, like "Within six months, I'll be with my Mr. Right." You can list specific details about who Mr. Right is, such as:

- ❤ Tall

- ❤ Blue eyes

- ❤ Salt-and-pepper hair

- ❤ An entrepreneur, a president or CEO of a company, a partner in a law firm, a CPA, or an architect in a major firm

- Over fifty

- Been married before

- Has two or three grown children

- Is very healthy and likes to exercise

Ask for specific things. You can even drill down to, "He loves to eat delicious food." (What does "delicious food" mean? It means Asian/ Fusion, French, or Italian food, or whatever you think is delicious.) Or "He loves my cooking and drinks fine wine," and then write down specific details—what you will cook for him, what kind of wine he drinks, etc.

I even got specific with my own needs and wants. I have a lot of hobbies and interests because I ski; I'm an avid golfer and tennis player; I love doing needlepoint, working out, and taking care of my pets; I'm an avid runner, philanthropist, animal activist, and real estate investor; I love hosting dinner parties, working, creating fundraising events, helping those less fortunate, and living life to its fullest.

Therefore, I wanted the person I was looking for to be as excited about life as I am, and not to be a couch potato every single weekend watching football or whatever it is. There's nothing wrong with that, but I wanted somebody who is active, has high energy, and has interests in lots of different things that are in alignment with my interests and hobbies.

But you also want someone who shares your core values, which all comes down to the manifestation letter. An example would be the business plan I just told you about. Successful entrepreneurs or companies first start with writing a business forecast plan for what they want to accomplish, and then they work backwards.

If what you want to accomplish is to find Mr. or Mrs. Right, you want to find a happily-ever-after relationship. Whether or not you're married, it's a committed relationship, so you work backwards by asking, "How do I get that and what does he look like?" Look at him like he's sitting in your living room, family room, or at your kitchen table, and you're reading newspapers and having coffee together. Or maybe you're walking down the beach together.

So ask yourself, "How does that actually feel?" Are you with him or her and you're both really connected? Or are you with this person hoping he or she is going to change? To get to Mr. or Mrs. Right, you have to go through Mr. or Mrs. Next, so you work through a lot of different people and ask questions. The more questions you ask before you give up your heart, the better. That way, if you find that person isn't compatible, you can cut him or her loose.

Peter: Renée, I know you've helped a lot of people. But even in your own particular circumstance, Jim isn't an avid tennis player or skier, so he doesn't have all the hobbies and interests you have. But he has some of them, correct?

Renée: Yes.

Peter: So what you guys really have is that connection.

Renée: We have an emotional and spiritual connection. No, he doesn't ski, but he'll meet me at the hotel where he'll be drinking hot toddies in front of a fireplace.

Peter: Well, that's how he connects with you on a hobby.

Renée: When I play tennis, he'll sit on the sidelines watching me play, so that's how we do things like that. We do things together, like while he's watching football, I'll be in the room with him doing something else. We still connect because we love each other, but we really like each other as well. The glue to a relationship is really enjoying hanging out together with that person, like he or she is your best buddy.

Peter: It seems like you may not have to share all the same hobbies and interests, but you better have that connection.

Renée: Correct. And that connection starts with your values and beliefs—the glue that binds your relationship together. A connection isn't just, "Oh, this feels good." You have to know what "good" means. It's chemistry and all these things that link back and forth to your values and beliefs, and you'll know when it feels right. Then it goes into the secondary level of your hobbies and fun stuff you want to do together.

The other thing that's really important in that connection is not just great sex (although that can be exciting and fun), but there's more to it than that. If both people have the value of family, it's important to link everything together. However, unless your family is so dysfunctional that you're not anything like them, you have to cut that tie and create boundaries so they don't negatively affect your relationship.

Peter: Going back to this whole notion of breaking old habits so you don't find Mr. Wrong again, an extreme case would be a woman who returns to a relationship with an abusive man. I know you have the manifestation letter, but how does a man or a woman break those old habits? Can you suggest some kind of reminder system not to get involved with Mr. or Mrs. Wrong?

Renée: Read what you wrote in your manifestation letter twice every day, once in the morning and once at night. Re-read it and work on it; re-read it and work on it.

Peter: You just told me to write forty or fifty pages, so how in the heck am I going to read that much every day? Is there a way to boil it down?

Renée: You can boil it down to writing a few key things in blue ink (like a blue felt-tip pen) on three or four 3x5 index cards. You can write some of the most important key values and beliefs that, in this case, will keep you from repeating old patterns. As an example, say you were attracted to an abusive relationship. This should be Step #1: Awareness of Old Habits. Step #2 is Look at Your Values—the ones you created in Chapter 1: Knowing Yourself. Look for the value that speaks directly to the opposite of your old habit. It might say, "I value safety in my life." Focus on that value. Write it in a form that applies to your ideal mate like, "My man/woman is kind and provides safety to our relationship." Write this on a minimum of five 3x5 cards and tape them in places that will remind you of what you want. You may tape them on your bathroom mirror, on your laptop, on your stirring wheel in your car, anywhere that will be a reminder of what you need and want in your life. Put that manifestation statement on your laptop screensaver, your phone, everywhere that will keep you in conversation with your unconscious self.

An abusive relationship should not be taken lightly. Normally, when you want to change an unwanted old pattern, the best way is to interrupt that pattern with outrageous, gregarious, out-of-your-comfort-zone action. It can be something as simple as a rubber band on your wrist that you snap every time you have a thought about calling, texting, or IM'ing Mr. Wrong. This is called aversion therapy, and it's a great way to keep your awareness sharp. Also, as you snap that rubber band, say out loud what you do want. In this case, say, "My ideal mate is kind and provides safety to our relationship." The more you focus on reviewing your own values, re-reading your manifestation letter, and noticing note paper with manifestation statements placed around your environment, the sooner you'll be with the person of your dreams, finding love at last and the connection for which you've always yearned.

Peter: So the most important things you're looking for in a connection are what you want to use as your filter.

Renée: Exactly. Take those forty or fifty pages and bulletpoint them on three or four 3x5 index cards. Read them first thing in the morning, and then read them before you go to bed at night. Those times are important because your mind is in a very suggestible place then and will give less resistance to your own commands. This repetition will embed them into your unconsciousness so they will come to fruition when you're awake during the day. You can even post and keep a set of them in your car as extra support to your goal.

Peter: That's really good. Actually, you talked about this as it relates to a business plan. When Jim and I work together, we talk about that as the "chief aim." So those chief aims are really those chief connection points and your intention to find the exact person you're looking for. Is that kind of what you're getting at?

Renée: Exactly. And thank you for saying that. It's living your life with intention and purpose because if you live your life with intention and purpose, you'll find your Mr. or Mrs. Right.

If you go through life just hoping you're going to find the right person, it may or may not happen (most likely it won't happen). You'll repeat the same pattern of falling in love with the wrong person again, and you'll waste a lot of time, or worse, you'll end up in an abusive relationship.

You can always make money, but you can't make time. We all have only twenty-four hours in a day, so you need to find the right person now. You can't be hoping he's going to marry you, or that he's going to fall in love with you, or that he's the right person, or that he'll please your family. You have to do it within yourself authentically and do what feels right.

Peter: Or hoping that he or she will change.

Renée: You can't change people because they are who they are. If they're over eighteen, they're not going to change. Period.

Peter: That makes a lot of sense.

Renée: Let people be. There are millions of people out there, so you'll meet the right person.

Peter: This goes back to Chapter 1: Knowing Yourself, where you said that to really know yourself, you have to be happy with yourself. And then you're able to go through your system of identifying all the things in the manifestation letter and boiling them down to your chief aim and intention to find that right person.

But if you don't have yourself where you want to be, and you are happy by yourself, to me it seems like you're always coming at it a little bit from a handicapped situation.

Renée: "Handicapped" is a great word. Or you're coming from a place of desperation. *Oh, I'm by myself. Therefore, if I'm by myself, something must be wrong with me.* Or you're the single girl coming without the plus-one to the party all the time, and you feel awkward.

Just be comfortable in your own skin, which is where you've got to love yourself and have self-confidence. When you have self-confidence, you're going to have tons of dates because confidence is what attracts people to people. When you're confident and have a little strut—and know you love yourself (not being in love with yourself, but loving yourself and knowing that you're worthy)— you can find anybody you want.

Peter: Before we wrap this chapter up, what's the difference between loving yourself and being in love with yourself?

Renée: Self-fullness versus self-ishness. Self-fullness is taking care of yourself in the sense of looking at yourself as being worthy and knowing that you can take care of yourself. You don't need to have somebody to make you whole. You're whole by yourself—you're not one-half of a person.

Peter: So this goes back to the whole idea that you shouldn't look for someone who's your ideal mate just because you're lonely.

Renée: If you're lonely, or you need to feel complete by having a relationship, then the person you find to have a relationship with is just enabling you.

Peter: That makes sense. Well, we're going to wrap this chapter up and move on to the next chapter where Renée is going to be talking about "Knowing Where to Find Mr. or Mrs. Right," which will get into things like what are the next steps in finding the ideal mate, and where you can find him or her.

Now that you've got this down and are focusing on your manifestation letter, it's time to start sowing the seeds to look for that ideal person you'd like to spend the rest of your life with.

Summary:

The same process that attracts our love at last is the same process that attracts Mr. or Mrs. Wrong. Even if we think or write down what we don't want, the energy and vibration that we send out to the Universe shows us what we do want. So the first step is to focus on what we do want by reading our manifestation letter at least twice a day, upon waking and before sleeping. These are the best times to imbed into our minds what we want to attract.

When we feel lonely and start to think about calling Mr. or Mrs. Wrong, that is exactly the time to read our manifestation letter and add intense emotion as we read it. No booty call is as important as our long-term happiness with our love at last. So stay the course and remain focused on what and who you designed for yourself.

Summary Questions:

Ask yourself the following questions:

Why do I keep repeating unwanted old patterns that attract Mr. or Mrs. Wrong?

_____

_____

_____

_____

_____

_____

_____

_____

_____

_____

_____

What can I do to break the old habit of attracting Mr. or Mrs. Wrong while I stay focused on finding the love of my life?

_____

_____

_____

_____

_____

_____

_____

_____

_____

_____

_____

_____

What steps can I take, based on what I've learned so far from reading this book, to interrupt these unwanted patterns and change the course of my relationship history so I feel confident that I'm going in the right direction for love?

_____
_____
_____
_____
_____
_____
_____
_____
_____
_____
_____
_____

Chapter 4

Knowing Where to Find Mr. or Mrs. Right

"When you stop trying to find the right man and start becoming the right woman, the right man will find his way to you."

— Author Unknown

"Finding love is like finding shoes. People go after the good-looking ones, but they end up choosing the ones they feel comfortable with."

— Author Unknown

Now that we've designed our perfect mate, it's time to determine where to find him or her. In this chapter, we'll discover that knowing where to find Mr. or Mrs. Right requires more than going to a place online or offline; it's more of a state of mind. The act of searching and being clear on what you're searching for will turn on the reticular activation system to attract Mr. or Mrs. Right to you. With so many places, opportunities, events, and websites available to us, it's really a matter of picking one and taking action.

So let's dive into this next chapter to find out where to find our love at last.

Peter: Renée, let's begin by discussing the many online and offline places to look for people to love. Although these sites claim that people connect and have marriages, we still have almost a 60 percent divorce rate in this country. I don't know whether these sites track that, but I'd be very interested in learning whether these online systems really work to keep people together.

I'd be very suspect of that because if people aren't doing the work that you're teaching people to do, they're still going to have a high chance of falling out of that relationship and having to go back to square one.

I think some of your readers by this point might be thinking, "Okay, so I've read these other chapters, but why couldn't I have just started with this one? Why couldn't I have just jumped on an online site, put up my profile, and started dating people?"

I think the answer is that just because you have an easy online tool where there's a whole bunch of people hanging out doesn't necessarily mean it's going to get you to your goal of finding the perfect mate, so maybe you can begin by speaking to that.

Renée: That's correct—I attracted 2,874 men to my Match.com profile, but all I wanted to attract were six to eight good candidates with the possibility of finding that one love at last. Even I had to go back and re-post my profile and description of whom I wanted to attract because I was attracting too many people. I know what some of you may be thinking, "Boy, that's a good problem to have—that many hits of possible lifemates!" But it isn't really a good situation if you think about managing that many love leads! It was insane at the beginning. I felt like I had been dropped in a tank full of hungry piranha fish and I was the new item on the menu! It takes lots of time to manage that many love leads, which is why I chose to readjust my profile and wants list. I knew if I could knock out some of the people who would be obvious non-candidates, that would be a good thing for me. The point I'm making is that this is not a popularity contest where the winner is the one with the most numbers. This is about finding the right person for you, period!

In fact, one of my love clients experienced just that; she followed my process to a T. She discovered who she was through her values and beliefs. She then wrote her detailed manifestation letter to God with blue ink on white paper in her journal. Then she posted herself on JDate.com and proceeded to get one and only one hit. But that one person who was attracted to her profile and her wants list was the one! Yes, he was her Mr. Right, and that's all that mattered—not how many men liked her or viewed her profile. No, on the first try, she hit pay dirt, four cherries across, walk-off home run, and hole-in-one. I think you get the idea. After all, that is what you and anyone else who uses this process wants—to find Mr. or Mrs. Right. And if you can do it right out of the gate, then great, go for it. And just to remind you, she did put in her dues to deserve this guy. She took her time to build her foundation of whom she was then, and from that action, she was able to be crystal clear about what and whom she wanted to manifest.

So what did my love client do that I didn't do to get a phenomenal result like that and so quickly? Well, for starters, she had an awesome love coach! But seriously, I had many mentors in the area of personal development and relationship building like Dr. Ava Cadel and Dr. Barbara De Angelis. But I had no one to guide me through this process that I created. In fact, the reason I attracted so many men first time out was because I was very clear on who I was—that came across loudly in my profile. From the work that I did with my mentors, I had a very clear understanding, feeling, and vision of who I was to me and the world. Many men are attracted to a woman who is confident and can express it without sounding bossy. My challenge was that I had no love coach who would have stopped me before I posted what I wanted to attract. Because my manifestation letter was so huge and I tend to be a very private person, I didn't put out an accurate description of whom I wanted.

Now a short bit of my love history. Before I came up with this love at last process, and before I spent the time and money to learn about who I was through my personal development mentors, and before it became socially acceptable to look for your ideal mate through the Internet, I would do what some of you may have done in the past—I would tell my friends that I was looking for the right guy or I would hire a dating service/matchmaker. I used that method to find those nine multimillionaires whom I got engaged to but eventually broke up with before it was too late. I realized then what you are probably realizing now—that no one—and I mean no one—can find and prepare you for the love of your life except you! I was what those expensive Beverly Hills matchmakers would call "a catch," and each and every guy I was put together with looked perfect for me on paper. But it doesn't matter what the paper says; what's in your heart and what your gut feels is what matters.

So I came to realize that going through matchmakers, dating services, and even high-end online dating websites didn't matter. I had to know myself first and then what I wanted before I could begin my search or use technology and services to find Mr. Right. There was no process out in the world that could get me the love of my life. So I made it! My only flaw was that I didn't have a coach to guide me, but that doesn't have to happen to you because I am here in your corner, to hold your hand through the process and help you find the right person for you.

So, yes, Peter, you are absolutely right; you'll just start dating people and you'll get whatever is out there. It's a waste of time if you're looking for that right person, but you have no idea who he or she is. Like I said earlier, you can always make money, but you can't make time. It's pointless, it's futile, you get bored, and you lose interest. That's why some people say, "I only find losers on dating sites" or "All of the good ones are taken." You're finding losers because that's what you're attracting. You're not manifesting what you want.

You can't just think about it or talk about it with your girlfriends or your buddies; you literally have to write it down. Yes, it takes a bit of work, but what's your life worth? That's where the self-love comes in versus being in love. Self-loving is knowing what you want and finding your purpose.

Sorry, Peter. I know that was a long answer, but I felt that it needed to be said.

Peter: No problem. I'm sure the readers felt your passion on this point, and if they skipped ahead to this chapter, now they'll go back and do the work and put in the effort to complete the earlier chapters in order to be ready for what we are about to get into here.

Renée: Yes, I hope so. It never works to put the cart before the horse.

Peter: This gets back to what you were talking about in Chapter 1. The first thing is you really have to know yourself before you can write down whom you want in your ideal mate, right?

Renée: Right. You have to know who you are and be very authentic and true to who you are if you want to attract your right mate. So whether it's from a website or in a parking lot at a drugstore or grocery store, you're going to attract the right person because that's what you're putting out to the Universe.

Peter: I find all kinds of mates in the Walmart parking lot—it just works out that way for me (just kidding). But I hear what you're saying.

You've mentioned that you need to understand and know your authentic self. One of the questions I've always asked (and you have it down here) is: How do you introduce your authentic self to the world of your ideal partner?

Renée: Well, first of all, be the person you've outlined that you want to be from the work you've done in Chapter 1: Knowing Yourself. Your values and beliefs become your code of conduct in the world. How you think, how you act, how you express yourself is by knowing yourself through your values and beliefs. When you are congruent with your values and beliefs, you can stand tall with confidence about exactly whom you'd like to present to the world as the authentic you. Earlier in Chapter 1, we talked about how some people will think one of their values is health. But they don't practice being healthy in their own lives. They don't show up in the world this way through their words, how they look, and how they act. When you act and show up incongruently to the value you stated, the only way to correct that is either to accept that health is not one of your values and is more of an interest or to be that value to yourself and the world. You don't have to look like a model or run like a world class marathoner to hold health as a value, but you need to show it, feel it, and be it to be congruent.

So once you're congruent with your values and your actions, it becomes easy to bring that out to the world because you are authentic. Then you don't have to act the part of being a person of health because you are a person of health. You're not a pretender but an accurate depiction of who you are.

So your ideal mate will not only see that value in your physical sense and hear it in your conversations, but he or she will feel it from the energy you give off; you are a lot more transparent than you think. You might be able to fool a few people some of the time, but not for very long. That's why it's important to take your time to get to know your ideal mate—to experience the person in different situations. When the heat is up, like certain social situations and events like birthdays, weddings, and holidays, the real you will always appear and the pretender will be exposed. But if you're accurately matching "who you are" with "whom you want," the love of your life will feel it in the energy that radiates around you, and you will get that from him or her as well.

Here's an example of being your authentic self: If you like to cook and you want to attract someone who enjoys cooking, you can find really great people at cooking classes. So just do a Google or Yelp search for: "Cooking classes in my area." So your authentic self loves to cook, loves the whole process and ceremony of cooking and eating, and knows it's important to your life. You may meet someone in the class who sees cooking the same way you do. From watching how he handles his ingredients to how he plates his culinary creation and how he sounds as he describes his dish to the class, you will feel his energy. People's passion and actions will show whether they are true to themselves or they are pretenders.

Now if you don't find the right person in this class, you may find people who are already married. But they know people, so they could be a huge influence with people they know and a resource for finding the person you seek. By being your authentic self in this event, you will show others not only who you are, but help them to know who will be the best match for you from their network of single and available friends.

Become friends with lots of different people, not just single people. You'll meet people at dinner parties; you'll get invited to different restaurants and other places. Sometimes, people like to do restaurant hopping, so you can go to a different restaurant every weekend with people you just met. So keep your circle of friends wide, and wherever you meet people, remember that they know people. The key is to be your authentic self always and to read your manifestation letter continually. Our five senses pale in comparison to the power of the RAS, so when you are out there among other people, they become your conduit to their network, which will be influenced by the power of your manifestation letter and RAS.

One of the tips I have on finding people is instead of only going on different online websites, tell all your friends and family that you're available and ready to date. You don't have to tell them about the manifestation letters or anything like that. But you will be attracting the right people through them. If it doesn't work out, don't blame that person for introducing you to the wrong person. You're putting it out there and the other person is doing you a favor. Just be your authentic self always.

When you're introduced to a potential partner, talk on the phone first; then meet that person and have coffee. Maybe go on a first date if you feel it's worth it to check out the person. One of the things I warn people about is, "Don't go to a movie on a first date."

Peter: Why is that?

Renée: It's two hours of time where you're not talking to that person.

Peter: A good point for guys.

Renée: Then you don't have to spend ten bucks per tickets. It's not that you have to be cheap. But if you spend ten dollars over coffee or a cocktail, you can learn more about somebody in two hours than you can at a movie. Of course, it's nice to discuss the movie. But the movie is not about your relationship; the movie is about the movie.

Peter: You've talked about a lot of places where you can find your ideal mate. (We'll get into some of the online sites here in just a moment.) But I'm still trying to understand how to introduce your authentic self to the world of your ideal partner.

For example, I'm a guy who has done this work and I really know myself, and I know what I'm looking for in an ideal partner. Let's say I invite a prospective mate out for a cocktail. I'm not going to jump into talking to her immediately about my value systems and all this kind of stuff because that comes over time. It would be really awkward if I'm going out with a woman for the first time and in the first five minutes, I ask her, "Do you want to have a family? How many kids do you want?"

So can you give us some tips on how to start conversations to get into a deeper level discussion where the authentic self can come out and you can ask about values and things like that?

Renée: You don't ask those questions at first, but you can pepper them into a conversation. So let's take the value of family as an example. Are you in front of the person for coffee or cocktails? Or are you on the telephone?

Peter: I invited her out for a drink, so we're face-to-face.

Renée: Then you may say, "What do you do for work?" She replies that she's a secretary or a teacher. "That's great," you say. "What grade do you teach?" Again, keep all the questions directed to that person, and link it to your values without him or her knowing you're doing that. Don't bring up the words "values and beliefs" to a new person because I'm using them just for the purpose of this book and to have as a tool for you to identify why you're going toward happily-ever-after.

Say she's a teacher. The conversation might go like this: "What grade do you teach?" "Second grade." "How long have you been a teacher?" "Five years." "Second grade? Those are cute kids. You must meet a lot of parents." "Yes, I do." "Have you thought about having kids?" If she says, "Yes," you can say, "How many do you think you'd have based on your working with kids every day?" So you're not saying it directly.

Let's say you're a guy who's Catholic, and you want to have two or three children. She says, "I only want to have one." Then the conversation could go like this: "Why would you like to have only one?" "Well, my parents are Jewish. It was a really bad relationship and they fought." So far, without being too obvious, you've found out some key facts: she works as a teacher, she only wants one child, she was raised Jewish, and she grew up in a tumultuous environment. All of this within minutes of sitting down for a cocktail for the first time. Oh, and the obvious—she enjoys a cocktail. So now you've gotten an idea of some of her beliefs. By spending some more time with your date and asking more questions, you'll even be able to come up with a value or two from your conversation.

So going back to your example, you're Catholic and you come from a loving family of ten brothers and sisters. But this woman you're having a cocktail with only wants to have one and she was raised Jewish.

There's nothing wrong with different religions, but you have to be aware of the differences that could be huge in their belief systems. Catholics historically tend to procreate and create large families. That's not to say that Jewish people don't enjoy large families. But if she were raised in a family where there was conflict and people were constantly arguing, even though your date may have said she wanted to have one child, she might be really gun shy about having any kids and making a commitment because of all the bad baggage from her rough childhood.

In addition, let's say both of you are in your late thirties, and even though she's still young enough to have a child, it's getting kind of dicey for her to have multiple children. So with you wanting two or three children and coming from a large family, that should be a red flag that this relationship might not work because children are important to you, your family, and your belief system.

Peter: I think it would be a big red flag and be really tough, especially if you are Catholic.

Renée: There's nothing wrong with people dating who are from different religions or have different spiritual beliefs as in this example. But the conflict is already there on the first date. Because you took the time to know who you are and what is important to you, now you are able to evaluate your next step quickly. You're not just intoxicated by her beautiful looks or her flowing hair; you're paying attention to what is really important in a committed relationship.

Now most people who don't follow this process would wait until the fifth, sixth, or eighth date to get to this realization, so they're shelling out money for those dates in a relationship that's not going to go anywhere. And while you're wasting your time on six meaningless dates, you could have been developing a relationship with the love of your life. That's why it's so important to have your values and beliefs in line because subconsciously you're thinking, *I'm a thirty-nine-year-old guy, and I want to have two or three kids, and she only wants to have one? This isn't going to fly.*

The issue of dual religions in the household won't even need to come up because not having two or three kids is a deal breaker for you. (Remember the list that you made, "Musts, Maybes, or Never.") Maybe she's a devout Orthodox Jew and you're a devout Catholic. You'll never get to that issue because your first "must" of having two or three kids will never happen with this person. Like I said, there's already conflict, so you probably should end that date within a half-hour.

Peter: You drink your cocktail and get out fast!

Renée: Or tea or coffee. Now I'm going to change up the scenario a bit and take it a little further. Let's say you're both Catholic and you're having drinks.

She tells you she's a teacher and loves children. You've both come from a large family and you want to keep that tradition going. She wants five, six, or seven kids—what would be considered a large family to you too. The problem is she's in her late thirties and she's ready to have children now, but you were expecting to spend a few years as just the two of you so you can explore each other and travel. So what do you do? She wants a big family and you want a big family, so the match is getting closer. Now, even at this juncture, you have to decide whether that belief about having a few years to yourselves is more important than finding your possible ideal mate and continuing the dating and evaluation process. What's the answer?

This is why doing your homework from Chapter 1 is so critical. You'll be experiencing these examples yourself all of the time, so you need to be ready. You could go either way on this example. You could decide that yes, this extended honeymoon time is very important to you and is tied to one of your values: celebration. Your belief is that an extended honeymoon period will cement your marital bonds with each other, preparing you both for the intensity of what a large family brings to the table. On the other hand, you may see the value of getting right to it and, immediately after you marry, begin the process of having a large family. You still value celebration, but your belief of an extended honeymoon period changed because having a large family is far more important and the celebration of many children was much more appealing by comparison.

So both being Catholic and such devoted church-goers, the glue bonds faster and is more long lasting than it would be with some-one who isn't spiritual or doesn't belong to an organized religion.

The point is to have something in common that you're doing on a regular basis that matches your values and beliefs and will keep you authentic to the real you. You attend church on Sundays; it's a routine, and it feels good because you've been doing it since you were a child, so it also brings back those basic family values, and now the possibility of bringing this to your own large family makes it more exciting to you—all because you are being your authentic self.

Peter: In my mind, those are very obvious examples. But what about things that aren't so obvious like emotional connection, physicality with sex, or things like that? How do you reveal your authentic self when you're having those conversations?

Renée: It's not so much how I reveal myself as it's more like extract-ing information from them. We'll talk more in the next chapter about probing questions and peppering conversations. But I like to use the example that once you do find someone who, on the surface, could be your ideal mate, you need to do what I call the "relationship mountain." Each time you get together, you're going forward up that mountain only to reach various plateaus. In devel-oping a long-term relationship, you have to know that you're not reaching the summit right away. Breathe and enjoy the process. Every time you reach a new plateau in your relationship, look to see whether the view is still great; if it's not, well, get off that moun-tain. If it's getting better, then keep on trucking. Love is a journey, not a destination to say you've finally arrived at. To this day, I still find that even with Jim, the journey is continuous and revealing. I am happy to continue this journey with him and travel hand-in-hand up to the next plateau.

So let's talk about that physicality with sex for a moment. If, for example, you're a guy, maybe you love to have sex twice a day, six times a week (even God rested on the seventh day). But you meet a woman who only likes to have sex once a week. (I'm going to get into something deeper than just physicality here.)

Peter: I hope you're going to tell me how to find out the woman only wants to have sex once a week.

Renée: There's nothing wrong with once a week or once a month—it just depends on what's right with that couple. And it depends on how comfortable you are in your relationship as you're moving through the relationship and up to another plateau.

Now this is a little bit deeper than the dating part because you might not be talking about sex until the third or fourth date. One way to broach the subject is to start asking questions like, "What was your ex-husband like?" Let's say she was married to her ex for only two years. "Oh, that's too bad you got divorced—that's such a short time. Do you mind if I ask what happened?"

People usually get divorced because of sex or money or both. I know that's very cliché, but from my interviews with my clients, it always seems to boil down to a lack of sex or a lack of money in a marriage as the symptom to a mismatch of values and beliefs. Somebody was fooling around (the sex). Somebody became a loser by being an alcoholic and lost all his or her money. Or someone was gambling in the casinos or was a day trader on Wall Street (the money).

Maybe she says something like, "My husband wanted sex twice a day—sometimes three times—every day and I just couldn't handle it. I only wanted it once a week, but all he ever thought about was sex. He wasn't making any money, but he always wanted to be in the bedroom. I couldn't handle that."

Let's say you're a guy who likes sex once a day. When you hear her say that, you know sex probably won't happen as often as you like since this woman only wants to have it once a week. Let's say you have fantasies and fetishes, but she only wants the basic missionary style, so it's not going to fly. You can kind of slip in a probing question here and there to find out what she likes.

Peter: Like "Would you like to spank me?" That might freak her out.

Renée: Peter, listen to this: When I was dating, I learned, "Many a true word is spoken in jest." If a guy is online, but I've yet to meet him, and he writes, "I'd love to go out with you. You're pretty. Let's go walk on the beach. Do you like dogs?" and I reply, "Yeah, I like dogs," and then out of nowhere, he writes "I'm really into sucking on toes." Oh-oh....

Peter: They would actually do that?

Renée: They would have written it to me online before I talked with them on the phone. There's nothing wrong with that. But when you see it already written out, or he has his shirt off and he's not in good shape and he's not that attractive, that's a turnoff.

Even if you're a guy who looks great, you don't want to show a woman your abs (or your beer belly) because you think that's sexy. I deleted a lot of guys who did the sucking on the toes thing or had no shirt on. It was disgusting! Too forward, too soon. Now, that's just my deal, but it's not a cool thing to do when you're presenting yourself to the world.

Peter: But I think that's probably a lot of women's deal. I don't understand why guys would do that—it makes no sense to me.

Renée: For some reason, men think that's what a woman wants. Sucking on toes is just one little thing—there's a lot more elaborate stuff out there. You might be a simple all-American woman, but wearing high heels and a T-shirt once in a while can be kind of sexy to a guy.

The point is that when a guy talks about stuff like that and you're just not into it, that's a red flag unless you're into it. The movie *Fifty Shades of Grey* is opening a lot of people's eyes because stuff like that does happen. I know people who love S&M. Whether it's light with feathers or heavy with leather and bondage, sadomasochism does happen. There's nothing wrong with that as long as both people are in agreement that it's consensual. (I should probably write a book on this.)

Peter: You talk about this in your workshop, but something guys struggle a lot with (I'm not a woman, but I think women do too) is how to go through the conversational process over the first few dates so they can really connect with and express their authentic self to the other person.

From a guy's perspective, if on the first date a woman started rambling for a half-hour about how horrible her ex-husband was and what a loser he was, I'd say, "You know what? I'm done."

Renée: You'd say that's Miss Next. Or if a guy is rambling for thirty or forty minutes on what's wrong with his kids, his mother, and/or his ex-wife(s). Or he's fifty-five years old and he's never been married before, that's another red flag.

Peter: And he lives with his mom in her basement.

Renée: All those things are huge red flags for me. We're going from one extreme to the other. One complains about his family and the other lives with his mother. He's fifty-five and he's never lived by himself. Those are red flags, so just delete (if you're online) or quickly end the date. If you're on a date, you can have a friend call you after a half-hour into the date, or you can have your beeper go off like an ER Doctor to save you from further misery.

Or if an alarm goes off on your phone, you can say, "Sorry; I have another appointment—I've got to get going." Or if things are going well, you can say, "Sorry; I have another appointment, but I'd love to spend more time with you. Would that be okay?"

Peter: That's better than going to the restroom and disappearing. That's all good. The questioning process you've provided is a good start for people. You've done the work and you know yourself, and you know what you're looking for in an ideal mate. Now it's just a natural conversational approach to finding out more to determine whether that person is the right match for you.

Since this chapter is about where to find the ideal mate, and online dating sites are really popular today, let me ask, how does a person know which online site is best suited for him or her?

Renée: Pick four or five sites you want to go on (e.g., Match.com, or if you're Christian, there's ChristianMingle.com). Sometimes, a dating site will give you one or two months for free, so go ahead and check it out. Spend about three or four hours a week uploading photos and revising your profile.

I think when you revise your profile, you increase your ranking position, just like you would for SEO on the Internet. If you change a photo, your rank goes up again so it looks like you're a brand new member, so that's kind of a cool thing.

Peter: When you add things to your profile, you appear to more men or women, depending on whom you're looking for.

Renée: Exactly. Maybe you want to add a hobby, a fun thing you like to do, or a new photo.

Before we move on to the next topic, I'd like to talk about photos. You want to have a photo of just your face or a full body shot with nobody else in it. You could include your dog. But don't make your photos always be about your dog or your cat because it's only about you.

Peter: Just from a guy's perspective, I'll tell you a little secret for what men look for. If a woman has a lot of photos of just her legs and her toes, she's probably overweight.

Renée: I didn't know that.

Peter: That's a rule of thumb we go by. I don't know whether women have that same rule of thumb. But if you're only showing a head-shot, and shots of your legs and your toes by the pool, she may be overweight. I'm not saying overweight people are bad; I'm just saying that's a dead giveaway for a guy.

Renée: It's a red flag because if you're not willing to be transparent in your profile or profile picture, where else are you not being completely honest?

Peter: I think guys with no shirts on are ridiculous, and it's probably a huge turnoff for women.

Renée: It's definitely a delete, so don't bother to respond. I had over 2,874 guys, and I pretty much responded to every one of them. I deleted the ones who were on the kinky side, so I learned a lot. But there are a lot of great people out there.

Peter: There are some places where you shouldn't look; one place I would never look for someone is on Craigslist.

Renée: I don't think Craigslist would be a good idea. Craigslist has had a poor reputation as a pick-up portal focused on one-night stands. It also can attract some unsavory characters, which is the exact opposite of what you are looking for in your soulmate. Craigslist may be a good place to advertise for a used car or a job opening, but not for the love of your life. Stick to the reputable online dating websites that I recommend later in this book.

Peter: So stick more with these relationship-type online sites?

Renée: Yes, eHarmony.com, Match.com, ChristianMingle.com, JDate.com. In addition to online sites, would you like me to share a couple of physical places?

Peter: Yes, please.

Renée: I mentioned earlier about finding your authentic self, and finding that person in your environment who has your same lifestyle. If you like to cook, take cooking classes. If you like to play golf, a driving range is a great place because you can chat a little bit. However, if you're playing tennis, it's hard to chat with somebody.

Peter: I could think of all kinds of bad jokes about a golf range with golf balls. But I get what you're saying.

Renée: A golf pro shop or the driving range. A lot of Christian churches have singles mixers, and they'll give an age range. All-inclusive singles resorts or cruises are fun and are a huge thing, so those are great places to meet people.

Even if you meet people who aren't exactly whom you want to go out with, they may know people. Don't just blow him off because he's got a big tummy or whatever. If he's a good person—but he's attracted to you and you're just not into him—he may know someone. You never know whether the person you're talking to is a center of influence and knows people who may match your expectations, so always keep your options open.

Peter: You just mentioned you can meet people on cruises or at resorts. But then you have this whole complexity of a long-distance situation. How do you address that?

Renée: Meaning you meet somebody who lives far away, a long-distance relationship?

Peter: Let's say I met somebody on a Caribbean cruise. If I live in California and she lives in New York, it seems that's going to be a big problem. Or is it?

Renée: No, it isn't. I was engaged to somebody who was living in Hong Kong. He was American and worked for Nike at the time, and he was a basketball player. I lived in Beverly Hills and we had a good relationship. When he'd come into town, we'd visit and hang out together for a couple of weeks, and then he'd leave.

After a while, he wanted me to move to Hong Kong. I said, "I don't think so" because it didn't feel right at the time. I had too much going on with my real estate business and projects in the States. It just wouldn't have been feasible and wouldn't have been right, so I had to cut him loose.

Peter: Since you're a living example of what you're looking for to find Mr. Right, would his location have been something you should have thought of in the beginning? *If this progresses, is this really going to work if he asks me to move to Hong Kong?*

Renée: Exactly. This is why I broke up with him. I wrote this book and have done coaching and seminars to tell people about the mistakes I've made. But my mistakes or failures were an education so I'd know what to do the next time.

My next time was when I met my Mr. Happily-Ever-After whom I'm married to now. Because I knew that living in a foreign country just wasn't my thing, when I met my Mr. Happily-Ever-After, and he was living in San Jose and I was living in Beverly Hills, we decided that either he would move to Southern California, or I would move up to Northern California. We discussed it within the first three or four dates.

Peter: If that happens in a boat cruise-type situation where it wasn't just a physical fling and you're going to continue the relationship, if you've done the work and you're both feeling a connection, that's probably something that should be addressed in the first few discussions.

Renée: Exactly. I'd like to regress for a moment: When I was engaged nine times, I had never met anybody online. That happened before online dating existed, so these were people I met through friends of friends, high-end matchmakers, and the centers of influence of different groups of people. And that's how I met all the wonderful men I was engaged to.

When I met my Mr. Happily-Ever-After, I was ready to do whatever it took because I was ready to commit. Now, I wrote down the distance I was willing to move: "It's time so I've really got to buckle down. If it means I have to move to New York, Northern California, Miami, Dallas, or wherever this person is going to come from, I'm ready."

At that time, I was really ready. I looked in the mirror and said, "What am I doing wrong to keep attracting people who aren't fitting into my lifestyle? If he meets all my criteria for my values, beliefs, hobbies, and interests—and he's my best friend—would I be willing to move to New York or Miami?" When I asked myself that serious question, the answer was, "Yes, I would."

Peter: For people who are reading this book, what you're saying is when you're writing your manifestation letter, you have to ask yourself, "Would I be willing to relocate for the right person?"

Renée: Right. But if you say, "I just want to live in my community within five miles," it limits you and narrows the pool of possibilities. Saying "Only Southern California" still somewhat limits you. So you don't want to put boundaries on where you'll move to unless you've got to be near children from a previous marriage and you have strong ties with your family and you have to see them every weekend. Some people need that, so keep it in your town or within five, ten, or fifty miles.

When I looked at my lifestyle, I asked myself, "What's holding you back?" I answered, "Nothing. I can go wherever I want." I had no children; I had never been married (so no stretch marks or track record).

Peter: No stretch marks. I love it! So you had to address that in your manifestation letter, so to speak. And you decided that if you really had a connection with that person and he was your ideal life mate, you would be willing to make the move.

Renée: Yes. Or he would come to me. In my case, my husband came to me.

Peter: You discussed that on the first few dates with Jim: "If this progresses, one of us is probably going to have to move. Are you okay with that?" And he said that yes, he was.

Renée: I think we had that discussion on the fourth date because everything was linking and going perfectly. Our first date was almost a five-hour lunch.

Peter: Wow!

Renée: Before that, we had talked offline on the telephone two to three hours a day, so we kind of already knew each other. I was in Beverly Hills and he was in San Jose, but our connection was already manifesting into a relationship on the phone. I didn't even know what he looked like.

Peter: I totally understand. It was two or three months before Patricia and I actually met face-to-face because I was traveling to Seattle so much. We did a lot of texting and talking on the phone to get to know each other.

But when it got to the time when we finally met, it amplified even more in a positive way.

Renée: Isn't that great?

Peter: It's very great.

Renée: Then you gave her a big kiss.

Peter: Yes. I took the chance and gave her a kiss the first time she opened the door. I think I surprised her, but it worked out.

Renée: Did you have a bunch of flowers for her?

Peter: For our first face-to-face date, we went to the town where she lived and we had coffee. But I bought her some flowers at the farmer's market and gave them to her there. She seemed to like them, so it was good.

Renée: That's so romantic. Are you planning something romantic for Valentine's Day?

Peter: Oh, yes. I already have something planned. She doesn't know about it, so it's a surprise.

Renée: I love surprises!

Peter: Renée, it's been really good learning about where to find Mr. or Mrs. Right. Not just about the locations, but about how you introduce yourself into the world of conversation. Thank you for all the information.

In Chapter 5: Choosing Your Soulmate, we'll discuss how you choose once you have a lot of people to choose from. Some good formulas and sequences for asking discerning questions will also be offered. Then we'll get into how to introduce your ideal mate into your community, tribe, or family. Finally, we'll talk a little about what is an appropriate amount of time to wait before you get married.

Summary:

The act of searching and being clear on what you're searching for will turn on the reticular activation system (RAS) to attract Mr. or Mrs. Right to you. With so many places, opportunities, events, and websites available to us, it's really a matter of picking one and taking action. Knowing Where to Find Mr. Right is more than going to a place online or offline; it's more of a state of mind. By continually reviewing your manifestation letter, you are always ready to receive your soulmate no matter where you are and what you are doing.

Chapter 4 Action Plan

Pick one online website to apply to for your search and one offline example that you feel comfortable using. You don't have to stick to the list provided in this chapter; these are just different suggestions to get you into action. You may find from your searching efforts some new, creative ideas for finding Mr. or Mrs. Right. If so, please feel free to share them with my Facebook community so we can all learn from each other. My Facebook community is: https://www.facebook.com/loveauthority/

Places, Circumstances, or Events for Finding Your Love at Last:

Remember, the whole phenomenon of online meeting and dating is fairly new compared to how it's been done for millennia. So here are some examples of creative and traditional places, circumstances, and events that create opportunities for you to find your Mr. or Mrs. Right, or at the very least, put you in action toward the direction you want to go. From your efforts of taking action, you may not meet your ideal mate in any of these ways, but what you're doing is telling the Universe, loudly and clearly, that you're ready for the love of your life. So when you pick an activity or event to attend, remember, "Ask and you shall receive."

Grocery Stores	Especially specialty or health-oriented grocery stores are best because they may be connected to one of your search outlines. People with health values tend to shop at better quality markets like Whole Foods, Sprouts, and Follow Your Heart. Or if you want your ideal mate to be Asian or appreciate Asian food and culture, you might try stores like 99 Market and Galleria Market.
Dog Parks or Popular Dog Paths	What better place to find your love candidate than through one of your "kids." Jim, since he's been with me, has said that he had no idea what having a dog with you can do to ease the process of finding a pretty girl—especially if it's a cute, small dog like one of our Malteses. It must be the natural maternal instincts that take over to make a total stranger come right over to you and begin to interact with you over your dog. So dogs become a natural conversation starter in all situations.
It's Just Lunch	Yes, this is a matchmaking service that specializes in putting you together with someone over lunch, but remember, you know who you are and what you want. So when you fill out a profile here, it will be a piece of cake!

Restaurants	Don't be afraid to go to a restaurant by yourself once in a while. It makes you more open to the opportunity to meet someone. But if you need a posse, go with people who don't look like your significant other. Especially if you're sitting in a fairly crowded or cramped restaurant, you can see what other people are ordering and comment on how good it looks to break the ice to a possible conversation. Remember, even if the person is not right for you or is currently unavailable, he or she has friends too!
Philanthropic and Charitable Events	Now we're really cooking! You may be attending a charitable event that benefits a cause you really believe in. Maybe your future Mr. or Mrs. Right has the same passion as you and he or she is just waiting to meet you. So say yes to that next charity function. The worst that could happen is a great dinner out and a tax write-off.
Charitable Walks and Runs	Now this could be a double bonus. Finding someone who is passionate about your cause and has a strong value in health. If you're a guy who has had a female member of your family who has been affected by cancer that primarily affects women and you're supporting her recovery by doing a charitable walk, what's the likelihood that a female walker will be there as well?

Ski Lift Lines	Well, lines in general are always an advantage. But ski lift lines are more focused on someone who likes at least one interest of yours, skiing, and possibly one value, health. So the next time you begin to complain about the long lines to get to the top, think opportunity.
Lines	Bank lines, grocery lines, ticket lines—you get the idea. You have a human who isn't too preoccupied or busy to talk, so what a great opportunity for a mini-conversation.
Golf Driving Range & Pro Shop	Hitting golf balls at a driving range can be a great place to connect with someone who is as passionate about the game as you are or is just passionate about being outdoors and active. There are times between driving the ball when you can get bits of conversation into the mix. And you can always meet up in the pro shop later to continue that conversation.
Film Festivals	Like I said earlier, a first date to a movie is not a good idea, but a film festival is quite different. You have parties, mixers, and lots of time between movies to connect with someone who may share an interest in the types of films being shown that day.

Baseball Games	The word on the street is that women go to baseball games to meet guys and guys like a girl who likes to be at sporting events. Besides, with all that time between innings and pitches, it's a great place that's conducive to conversation.
Volunteer Work	You'd be surprised who you'll meet at a volunteer situation. It's great networking in general, but wouldn't it be great to do some good in the world and meet the love of your life as a bonus. Jim and I would help feed the homeless once a month for a while. Most of the work is moving bags and packaged food from one part of the table to another so skilled help is not necessary. We noticed lots of pretty single girls who would have loved to meet a helpful male volunteer. (That's what we call a hint.)
Meetup.com	Meetup.com has a variety of events in a neighborhood near you. Once again, it's a great opportunity to stretch yourself by learning new things and meeting new people. Remember, it's about putting yourself out there in the world.

Apple Store	You'd be surprised how many people gather at the Apple Store to look, ask questions, and take one of the many free classes the store offers. Now, if you're a baby boomer looking for someone special, these free classes are mostly made up of people fifty years and older learning how to use the latest mobile gadget. If one of your top values is learning, intelligence, or continual improvement, well, you might be meeting someone who has similar values at one of these classes. The worst thing that could happen by going to class is that you'll learn about one more app you can put on your iPad.
Religious/Spiritual Singles Events and Outings	Every good-sized church will usually have a singles event planned every month or so. Agape—the non-denominational church run by Rev. Michael Beckwith in Los Angeles, California—has singles mixers on a regular basis, and periodically, it will have ski trips and other outings. The same is true for many other Christian churches, so if attending church fits within your spiritual beliefs, it could be a great opportunity to find someone who fits your profile. If you currently belong to a smaller congregation that can't support a single organization or the number of singles is too small to offer you much choice, look for a mega-church in your city that would be able to support such an organization.

Adult Learning or College Continuing Education Classes	Wow, this is a big one. You can potentially meet someone who shares multiple values and beliefs with you, and you also leave with an education. A win-win to me! I mentioned earlier in this chapter about cooking classes and meeting people there. Well, back in the day when Jim owned a restaurant and cooking school, every few months, he would offer a singles-only cooking class where the class was designed for everyone to have a chance to cook together before they all sat down to enjoy what they had made. Besides being lots of fun, these classes give you an opportunity to learn a lot about people's characters and personalities by observing them cooking and preparing food. In fact, Jim would share some of those personality traits with the class prior to starting to cook. Maybe if we're nice to him, he'll bring back that class during our next weekend Find the Love of Your Life workshop.

So bottom line, you can't find Mr. or Mrs. Right sitting on your sofa at home unless you think the UPS guy is your right match. Even online dating eventually puts you out into the real world. So commit to breaking some cocooning habits and get out there and see the world. Even if the love of your life is not out there yet, you'll have more fun being among the living!

Summary Questions:

Where is the right place to find my Mr. or Mrs. Right?

_____
_____
_____
_____
_____
_____
_____

Is it better for me to go to an online dating site or offline in the real world?

_____
_____
_____
_____
_____
_____
_____

Which is the best online dating site for me?

_____
_____
_____
_____
_____
_____
_____

What choices do I have to meet my ideal mate in person?

_____
_____
_____
_____
_____
_____
_____

How can I be my authentic self while looking for the love of my life?

_____
_____
_____
_____
_____
_____
_____
_____
_____
_____
_____
_____
_____
_____
_____
_____
_____
_____

CHAPTER 5

Choosing Your Soulmate

"Choose your love. Love your choice."

— Thomas S. Monson

*"It's not hard to make decisions when you
know what your values are."*

— Roy Disney

So congratulations! You are more prepared than 99.9 percent of
the people looking for the love of their life. So be confident that
with all of the work you've done, when you begin making these
choices, they will be the right ones for you.

Up until now, everything in this book has been about building the foundation to choose the love of your life. Well, the time is here to begin the process of evaluating and eliminating. If you didn't know it by now, you'll be eliminating more than putting people through to the next level. So get comfortable with being discerning in your decisions and listen closely to what is being said because now it's time to choose your Mr. or Mrs. Right!

Peter: In this chapter, we're going to be talking about choosing your soulmate. Renée, as we discussed in the last chapter, there are lots of places to find people. You mentioned that you had 2,874 guys contact you, but even for people who have 100 to 150, I think that's kind of a daunting number. So how would people narrow that list down?

Renée: Out of the 2,874 guys I received emails from, I went out on a preliminary meeting with only eighty-four.

Peter: Even that number must have taken a long time.

Renée: It actually didn't. Here's how I went out with eighty-four in just a few months: I'd schedule four to five dates or more at a Starbucks in Beverly Hills or Brentwood near where I lived. So it didn't look like something odd was going on, I'd tell the cashier that I was casting a movie, and I'd be interviewing men for a part. The truth was, I was interviewing men for a part, a part in my life as my love at last.

Peter: You were casting a movie? I love that.

Renée: And I told the cashier I'd be meeting five to eight men, one man every thirty to forty minutes. "I'm going to be holding this table for a few hours as my office," I said. So that's what I said, and, of course, all those men, plus me, were buying cups of coffee, so the cashier was fine with it.

I didn't want to say, "I'm looking to meet my future husband" because it would sound ridiculous. Casting a movie sounded more realistic, especially since in L.A., Hollywood, and Beverly Hills, almost everybody's about being in the film industry.

Before I interviewed them—before they got to that second tier—I looked at their profiles. If the man was a possible contender, then I'd take the next step and meet him in person.

Peter: Let's slow down for just a second. How did you get to that first cut where someone was a contender before you met him in person? What was going through your mind to make that cut?

Renée: I'm going to refer once again to values and beliefs. I only wrote short paragraphs in my profile, and on the bottom, I wrote what I was looking for. Would you like me to tell you what I wrote?

Peter: Yes, please. That would help.

Renée: I wrote that I was looking for somebody...

- ❤ Over fifty
- ❤ Who's been married once or twice
- ❤ With children over sixteen years old
- ❤ Who was an entrepreneur or corporate (e.g., a partner in a law firm, an architectural firm, or a CPA firm)
- ❤ Who would allow me to be me
- ❤ Who loved to eat delicious gourmet food and drink fine wine

That was about it. Because I could only write a limited number of words on my profile, I didn't want to talk about walking on the beach or horseback riding like you see many women write about in their profiles. I wanted the words I wrote to count. I just wrote those basic things.

Then on the profile itself, I listed things I like to do: skiing, golfing, tennis, and adventurous new restaurants—basic stuff like that.

Peter: Going through this initial selection process to pare it down, you wrote what you were looking for. Did you read each person's profile beforehand to see whether he had those things in there?

Renée: Yes. Like I mentioned in Chapter 4, if what he wrote was too risqué and I could tell right away it was quickly heading toward a sexual connotation (remember we talked about sucking on toes?), I'd delete it because I didn't want to waste time; that wasn't for me. I was getting 250 emails per day, so I had to create some sort of process to delete these people. (The white lettering on my keyboard's Delete button eventually wore out.)

At the time I deleted them, I would email each one back and say, "I'm so sorry. You're not the right one for me. But good luck with finding the love of your life, and God bless you." I'd type each message out because I didn't know how to cut and paste at the time (this was in 2000), send it, and then delete the person's profile. I'd try to do this consistently because I had to stay on top of it.

Peter: Out of the 2,874 men who contacted you, what would happen if you read their profiles and they had some things you were looking for but not all of them? Did you delete them right away?

Renée: No. I stayed open-minded if the potential was there—if they knew where they were going in their life—and their vocation was of some substance (e.g., they weren't still in college; they weren't in their twenties or thirties, etc.). I wasn't crazy about meeting a school teacher or somebody in a government job because I wanted more of an entrepreneur. But if they were in that realm of possibility, I still gave them an opportunity, so we'd go back and forth on emails.

Then I'd call them on the phone just to feel their energy and vibration. I'd listen to their tonality and how they enunciated certain words, and I'd ask them a few more questions. Then if I thought they were a possibility, I'd say, "Yes, let's meet for coffee."

Peter: You said you met eighty-four men for coffee. But how many did you talk to on the phone?

Renée: I talked to maybe 1,150 to 1,200.

Peter: How in the heck did you fit all that in?

Renée: I kept notebooks instead of journals. I wouldn't print everybody's profile, but for some, I'd write down his name and handle. For others, I'd print his profile (I used a lot of printer ink), and then cut and pasted; I literally got out the scissors and the Elmer's Glue-All and pasted his profile into a notebook so if he emailed me again, I'd know I had already talked to him.

Peter: Did you give yourself a time limit on the phone? Otherwise, this process would have taken months.

Renée: It took several months. This took place between April and October 2000. I'd have them call me and leave a voicemail message, and then I'd call them back. I had a private caller ID on my phone on purpose so they wouldn't know my number.

Peter: So you'd suggest getting a Google phone number?

Renée: It's now 2016, and there are Google account numbers where you can leave a phone number. But in the year 2000, there was only my message on voicemail, so they would leave a message and their phone number. I would never give them my number unless I felt comfortable. But yes, a Google phone number is a great tool that gives you a privacy cushion that I highly recommend.

Peter: Your experience is extraordinary. But I can't believe that an average person is going to call 1,200 people. So what's your advice for the person reading this book who's thinking, *There's no way in heck I'm calling 1,200 people to find my mate?*

Renée: You're absolutely correct, and that's why I'm writing this book. I obviously made mistakes and learned by my mistakes. I just happened to score a lot of men emailing me, which was very fortunate. I've heard from other people that they don't get as many. All I wanted was six or eight men to email me, and I was going to pick one and say, "Okay, this is a good one, and I'll have him as my husband."

Little did I know it was going to be almost 3,000 men, which I've heard from other people is more than usual. Like I said earlier in this book, a lot of credit to the success that I had in attracting love leads was that I had worked hard on myself to know who I was and what I wanted. It showed in my profile and how I was perceived. My husband, Jim, who was on the other end of my process, told me long after we were married that what he got from my profile was that I was very successful and very confident. Yes, my photo did get his attention and my exotic looks fit what he preferred in a life partner, but what prompted him to email me was the sense of confidence that he got from my profile. He said that was and still is a big turn-on for him. He made a commitment to himself not to attract women who needed fixing. He wanted a woman who knew who she was and walked the talk of who she was to the world.

Just a side note before we continue, Peter. I want to make it very clear that you don't have to be a former professional model like me to attract your Mr. or Mrs. Right. I want you to attract your right person, so that's why I encourage people to spend the time to be clear about what they want through their manifestation letters after they confirm their values and beliefs. But you do want to invest in a few great current pictures taken by a professional or at the very least someone who is talented in taking good photographs. My lead photo on my profile was taken by a very good professional, and I'm sure that contributed to my getting more attention than the average girl. But it was the profile that hooked the men into taking the next step to email me.

I had to create a process and a plan, so I created an outline of how to go about doing this.

Let's say 1,000 men email you. How do you do a process of elimination? I'm going to give a metaphor about how women go shopping to explain my plan. By the way, Peter, I may use cloth or shopping metaphors not just because I'm a woman, but because I'm also trained in the area of fashion design and was a graduate of the Parson's School of Design in New York. That's why I incorporate a personal fashion makeover within my protégé Gold Package Coaching Program.

Let's say there's a sale at Nordstrom or Neiman Marcus. And I give my hard-working assistant Jennifer a huge bonus of $5,000 to shop with (which isn't a lot of money if you're going to Neiman Marcus), but she gathers $20,000 worth of clothes in the dressing room to evaluate and consider.

She's going to try on the clothes, and she's going to feel them, look at them, and hold them up to her in the mirror. She's going to decide either to return each one to the rack or to keep it. She's going to go through the process of elimination because she knows herself, her body, and her colors. Most women know what colors look good on them (jewel tones, earth tones, fall/spring/winter, etc.).

The same goes for finding the love of your life. Knowing who you are is in your manifestation letter and values and beliefs. Beliefs can change because there are different links, but your values pretty much stay the same. There's a huge distinction because it's based on perception and perception always changes.

Sometimes we put so much meaning into certain things that we change the meaning of those beliefs. We create more certainties in other areas, but our beliefs stay the same. Does that make sense?

Peter: Yes, I understand. But going back to the process, let's say the average woman gets 150 contacts. So what's the process for going through them quickly so it doesn't take weeks or months?

Renée: I definitely believe that knowing who you are and where you want to go is going to help make your journey faster, so you create guidelines for yourself so you are very clear. If a man's profile has nine out of ten hobbies and interests you want—and four out of five of the same values—he has lots of potential. So I'd say email him or try to get him on the phone because it's better to listen to his tonality and articulation and then go from there.

Then you can ask him a few key questions in a certain sequence to get him to talk about himself. It's better to ask more questions than to talk about yourself, but in a way, he doesn't know you're interviewing him. All you're doing is carrying on a conversation about him, and most people like to talk about themselves, so that should not be a problem. When I say probing questions, what I mean is for you to come up with a minimum of five or six questions that will give you a good sense of this person to see whether he will qualify to go the next step. These questions are taken from your manifestation letter of what you're looking for in your life.

This is what I would ask in my search:

1. Do you believe in God?

2. Is family important to you?

3. Do you have a stable income or way of making money?

4. Is health important to you?

5. Whom do you love?

6.   Do you continually learn and improve yourself?

Now, I'm not looking to have all of these questions answered on one call, and I'm not looking to use these questions exactly as I have them written. I'm using these questions as a reminder or guideline to keep me focused. In fact, on every call I have, the probing questions will change depending on the conversation to keep it natural.

More importantly, once you begin the evaluation process, first from reading the person's email to you, then by reading his or her profile, then by having that first phone call and subsequent calls, you must use all of your senses to evaluate at each step whether the person gets a green light to go to the next level; a yellow light of caution so you proceed very carefully; or a red light so you stop and get off that mountain. Listen carefully with both your ears and your heart, and always go with your gut; listen to your intuition because that never gets fooled by all of those pretenders.

Peter: That sounds good. Now let's fast-forward and say some of them made the cut, so you plan for a face-to-face meeting and you're at Starbucks. You talked about getting to the heart of the matter through questions. Do you have a formula or sequence for asking good questions that help you to determine quickly whether this man or woman may be a good fit?

Renée: I'm going to go with my values as an example. My number one value is God, then family, financial security and stability, health, love, and finally, continuous personal development. Let's say you talk to this person before you go for coffee. You're talking about religion and you say, "Today is Sunday. Did you already go to church?" He says, "No, I'm an atheist. I don't believe in God. I just believe in science, and God never comes into the equation because I've been hurt before." For me, blaming God and religion and other things for whatever heartaches he's had is a red flag no matter what he does for a living.

If God is important to you, but he's putting Him down, it isn't going to work. Just forget about it. But if he believes in God and he just went to church, great. That's a green light and you get to go forward.

Then you might ask the person, "Are you going to see your family today? Do you visit your kids on the weekend?" If he says, "Oh, no. My son's in rehab, my ex-wife's an alcoholic, and my mother is crazy. They're the ones who created all this pain in my life," then you just hit a yellow light, so proceed with caution.

If he continues to go on and on, talking about himself for twenty minutes without ever asking you a question, my perception would be that he's self-centered. You already have drama in your life so you don't want more drama. Drama creates stress on a relationship as well in your body so you won't live long.

As a woman or a man, you're not in a relationship to fix the other person. You come together as two whole people—not for the other person to make you feel whole. Period. So this person hit a red light with you; get off that mountain before you endure any more negative energy and move on to the next prospect.

Peter: One of the suggestions that I think is buried in there is to ask open-ended questions because close-ended is a yes or no response. Open-ended questions are more about getting the other person to open up and talk to you so you can listen. Correct?

Renée: Correct. You want to have open-ended questions because you want to hear more about how the person feels about different situations (friends and family, religion or spirituality, animals, or even his or her job). In fact, try to focus your conversation around your core five or six questions that you've written down. Getting back to my God core value question, some conversational probing questions that would open up or continue my core value question might be: "How do you celebrate Easter?" Or if the person has kids, "How were your kids raised spiritually?" Or if the person is divorced or widowed, "How do you spend Sundays now compared to when you were married?"

Peter: You're obviously pretty good at having these conversations because you were able to narrow it down from eighty-four prospects to picking one individual (Jim). When talking about open-ended questions—and let's continue with the example of religion and belief in God—would I say, "How do you feel about religion?" How do I do that without making it feel like an interview?

Renée: You don't have to say the words "religion" or "spirituality." You can talk about something like a book or a movie. "Did you see that movie *The Secret*?" Or since it's 2016, something like "There's a big crisis now with ISIS, which believes it is doing Allah's work; what do you think about that?" You can create a question around a current event, but gear it toward your five or six core value questions.

Peter: We're going to talk a little bit about discerning questions. So is a discerning question where you're kind of leading the person down a path to discover what his or her belief or value systems are?

Renée: Yes. You want to lead the person on that path of those five to six values as soon as you can, but you need to create the questions first. Let's say you're in your late thirties or forties and you really want to have children. This guy is over fifty and has three kids, and for whatever reason, he definitely doesn't want to have kids. No matter what he looks like, or what he drives, or what he does for a living, that's a red flag and a moot point because you can't get into the relationship thinking you're going to change him. "I'll make him want to have kids." If he doesn't have kids now, and he doesn't want kids, he's not going to want to have kids in the future with you or anyone else.

But if a guy says, "I've been married and I've got three kids. I really missed listening to the pitter-patter of tiny feet because I was building my multimillion-dollar company and was always working when my first three kids grew up. I would love to have another family and have at least two or three more kids. If the person I marry can't have kids, I want her to be at least open to the possibility of adopting," then you know there's a possibility.

Pets are also part of the equation. If you're a real animal person, but he detests or is allergic to dogs and cats, learn that now. Or if you love horseback riding, but he's allergic to horses (though that's not much of a red flag because he can take allergy pills). But if he doesn't like horses because he just doesn't like animals, for me that's a major red flag, so you need to move on and stop wasting your time with this person.

Millions of people out there are single, so there's someone for everybody; don't settle for less.

Peter: That makes a lot of sense. Let's say you've narrowed your prospect list down to ten or fifteen people to have coffee with. Do you just let the conversation go as it goes with each person? Or do you have a time limit?

Renée: At the twenty-four or thirty-minute mark, it would be good to have a friend call or to have an alarm go off on your phone. You could say, "I'm expecting a really important phone call. Do you mind if I take it?" Or "I'm sorry, but I've got to call somebody back by this time." You can say it to be courteous, and it also gives you an out if you think time spent with this person isn't going anywhere. You can set an alarm at the beginning of the time with that person because it's the polite thing to do.

Peter: So your rule of thumb is to give each person about thirty minutes. And if things are going well and there are lots of green lights, then you continue exploring the conversation with that person.

Renée: Yes. But it also keeps you on point as well knowing you've only got about twenty-four minutes. Now, if that time is going quickly because you're having a great time, just say, "I'm having a great time, so let me postpone what I have to do." Then step outside and make a pretend phone call. Then that person will feel really good and think, *Wow, we're creating something really good here. Maybe this is a possibility for me; she may be the one.*

Peter: You wouldn't necessarily do the whole back-to-back every thirty minutes because then you're stuck with another guy coming and that could be very awkward.

Renée: You can do the back-to-back. But if another guy is coming, you can say, "I have to get going" because you've got six more appointments coming. It's just like a doctor. You have to keep your appointments on schedule because some people may be traveling from far away.

So you could say, "I'm really having a great time, but I need to get to this other appointment. Would you mind if we met for cocktails or lunch another time? Does that sound good to you?"

Peter: You can kick the person out the door before the next one shows up.

Renée: No, if it's a day that I'm interviewing five or six guys, which is a lot, I'll schedule each appointment one hour apart. Allow for a five-minute early arrival for each one. Start at the top of the hour and by twenty-five minutes past the hour, begin to decide whether this person is leaning toward a green light, yellow light, or red light. By thirty-five minutes past the hour, wrap up your meeting, and if it's a green light, make a plan right then and there with either another phone call, another Starbucks meet-up, or if it was really successful, maybe a lunch. If it's a yellow light, proceed with caution and just schedule a phone call to re-evaluate the situation and give the person one more opportunity. And if it's a red light, be honest and say that you're not interested in anymore meetings together.

The extra cushion of time should be about ten to fifteen minutes to accommodate early arrivals, and it should be used to write notes in your journal or notebook while the meeting is still fresh in your mind. The extra cushion of time is not just to prevent an embarrassing moment but also so you stay organized with your notes, which is easy to do. When I am pressed for time, I'll use a scale of 1 to 10 with a one word index like: appearance 9/10, conversation 8/10, engaged 9/10, God 7/10, family 8/10. The definition of this scale is his appearance was very good; he was handsome, had clean fingernails, nice cloths, and hair. Conversation was very good. He asked lots of questions and didn't avoid or question the questions I asked him. He was engaged or present in the conversation, meaning that his eyes were not wandering and checking out the other girls; he looked at my eyes most of the time and not my cleavage (not necessarily the type of engagement I would want). God means with regard to my core questions about God or creator how well he answered for the time we had for this meeting. This was his lowest score, but it was still over halfway so that would be a caution signal to be looked at later. Family means that he did well with my questions connected to my core question about family. So, overall, this person would get a green light and I would set up another date with him for coffee, drinks, phone, or lunch.

When I met my husband, Jim, we spoke for three-and-a-half to four weeks every day for two-and-a-half to three hours a day.

Peter: On the phone, or in person?

Renée: I was in Beverly Hills, and he was in San Jose. I had no idea what he looked like because it was the year 2000 and I didn't know how to go to a website. Don't laugh, but at the time, I didn't know the difference between an email address and a website address.

Peter: You didn't go through an online dating website?

Renée: I was on Match.com. He happened to go there because his friend, who happened to be above my profile, was getting zero hits. She had the wrong profile and tagline, so guys were saying, "I don't think so." He happened to scroll down and saw my picture. He read it and said, "Wow. She sounds interesting."

He emailed me twice, but each time it bounced back. My mailbox was too crowded because so many men were emailing me every single day. The third time he tried, it went through, so we started to talk and traded numbers.

I gave him my voicemail number and we talked back and forth. Then I gave him my real number and we started talking. When we finally met, our first date was almost five-and-a-half hours.

Peter: Wow! And this was all while you were talking to the other eighty-four men.

Renée: Yes. Until you get a ring on your finger, you're still available.

Peter: So you went through this process and kept notes where you kind of boiled it down to only Jim, your Happily-Ever-After.

You said your value system was God is first and family is second, so you probably wanted to introduce Jim to your family and your friends (you called it a community or a tribe). So what are some rules of thumb or advice on how to do that?

Renée: Because I've had so many boyfriends, I thought, *What's the point of inviting them to my home for an Easter, Thanksgiving, or Christmas dinner if they're not going to be around in six months?*

Peter: Your mom and dad were probably going, "Next...next...."

Renée: My dad always said, "Don't ever cry over a guy (he told me this when I was seven or eight) because, like a bus, there's going to be another one every five minutes." And I said, "Oh, okay. Got it." So I've never really cried over a guy.

I never intentionally hurt people or break it off with them. But I will if I feel it's not going anywhere or I'm bored (it's usually because I'm bored). Most of the time within three to four weeks—maybe six weeks at the most—somebody's asking me to marry him.

Peter: What was it about Jim that caused you not to be bored?

Renée: He became my best friend. He didn't tell me what to do, and he allowed me to be who I am.

Peter: But how did that keep you from being bored?

Renée: A lot of men I was attracting wanted to control me by keeping me as a bird in a gilded cage, and after a while, it just got boring. They weren't fun and they didn't make me laugh. They were plain white bread. Their controlling nature didn't allow any peaks or valleys, which became just boring and flat line emotionally. I'm not talking about tachycardia where your heartbeat is abnormally racing every time you're around this person. But some variety in emotions is what I preferred in a relationship.

So whenever Jim and I got together at a restaurant, it was always a three-and-a-half-hour dinner where we were always talking and laughing. To this day, sixteen years later, we're still talking and laughing like it's our first date. How can you be bored with that?

Peter: You bring up a really good point. You have values and beliefs, but obviously personality traits are very important. One of the things I'm hearing you say is you hold humor in very high regard as a personality trait, especially if someone is funny and can make you laugh. Is that correct?

Renée: Correct. And the other thing that's very important is respect for one another. Not only do Jim and I love each other, but we respect each other and are committed to the relationship. Humor is right up there, but we also put each other on a pedestal, if that makes sense. We praise each other to other people, and we take care of each other and our hearts. Things like that are what Jim and I have in common. In fact, I wouldn't be writing this book and helping people with their relationships through my coaching and seminar programs if it weren't for Jim. He is an expert trainer and coach in the corporate area focusing on team building and leadership development, so it's all about building relationships with him. He said that if he had not found me, he would have been the first person to buy my book, take my seminars, and be coached because there was nothing else available like what I do for people that produces real long-lasting results like my process produces. That's why I'm here with you today.

Peter: And we're glad you're here! The reason why I bring that up is going back to your manifestation letter, which is defined by your values and beliefs, but also by the personality traits you're looking for in the other individual.

I agree with you, too, that the process works because you obviously made the right choice. I know Jim really well. He's always funny, upbeat, and happy. I've never seen Jim have a down day in all the time I've known you guys.

Renée: Neither one of us have. We wake up happy, laughing, and giggling even before we get out of bed. We've got dogs climbing all over us, and our forty birds are yelling and screaming. We have five aquariums and a koi fish pond. It's a zoo, and it's fun and light.

We created this. It isn't like, "Oh gosh, it's Monday. What do I have to do?" When we put our feet on the floor, the first foot says, "Thank," and the second foot says, "you" (Thank you, God!). We're fortunate we have each other, our animals, our friends like you and

Patricia, our relationships with other people, and our home and our businesses. We're grateful every day, and we don't take anything for granted.

Peter: Just to put it on record for this book, I will personally attest that your house is a zoo, so it's good that you have a love for animals.

Renée: It is a bit much. Some of them are outside now because it's really sunny so it's a bit quieter, especially in the morning when they're calling other birds, saying, "Hey, wake up!" It's a "call of the wild" first thing in the morning and when the sun sets.

Peter: That's all good. That helped you find your match with Jim, and then when you introduced him to your family, the relationship progressed.

If you want to get married, is there a time when you should start thinking about marriage? Or should you just jump into it? Is there such a thing as love at first sight, and then "Let's just get married" a month later? Or should there be a period of time when you get to know that person?

Renée: I believe in love at first sight. It hasn't happened to me, but it has to people who wanted to marry me. So I just said, "Yeah, that sounds fine." The more I said, "No," the more they pursued me.

Peter: Then it's like a conquest—it's not necessarily true love.

Renée: I think I have more masculine than traditional female traits, even though if you saw my closet with all my clothes, you'd know I'm very feminine. Both Jim and I have strong personalities. Having men falling in love with me was kind of common, so it wasn't a big deal. *Like, whatever,* I thought.

Peter: Was there a period of time that you and Jim gave yourself? Or that you would suggest people give themselves before they think about becoming serious and getting married?

Renée: Jim and I wanted to have a relationship before we even met each other. I came to the conclusion that we were very happy being on our own forever. After we met and dated for six months, I knew he was the one. But Jim knew the day we met that we had huge potential.

What really got us to commit to moving toward marriage was when 9/11 hit. We didn't want to be without each other, and we wanted to be committed to the ceremony and the sanctity of marriage.

Peter: Obviously, marriage isn't for everybody. But let's say one person wants to get married and the other doesn't. How do you treat that situation?

Renée: You need to find that out within the first few weeks. Not during the first through the fifth dates, but you've got to have a direction. It's like having kids: If the person doesn't want to get married, but marriage is really important to you, you need to find this out before you fall head over heels for him or her and before you have sex.

Especially with women, when women have physical intimacy and have sex with a man, they become emotionally locked up; it's harder for them to break it off emotionally once they've given themselves to a man. That's why I always held off for as long as I could.

Peter: You're still probably holding off for Jim, right?

Renée: No, no, no!

Peter: I'm just kidding.

Renée: I see this in women all the time. It's better to be best friends with your vibrator than to have sex with somebody who's just passing through.

Peter: We're going to use that as a quote on the front of the book: "Love at Last...With My Vibrator."

Renée: Put your vibrator close to your heart instead of having guys just for a booty call. It's not a nice feeling if you have sex with somebody and it's just for the physicality of it because you end up feeling icky.

Peter: This information has been great. Thanks again for all your insight and advice, Renée.

In the next chapter, we will be discussing dating in the workplace, and then the final chapter will cover specific things like how to stay away from nut jobs and how to use social media. So stay tuned as Renée goes through some of her tips and tricks on working toward that final decision.

Summary:

In this chapter, "Choosing Your Soulmate," we discussed the process of evaluation and elimination so you can get closer to finding your love at last. We talked about how the choosing process is vitally connected to the foundational information that we discovered in Chapter 1: Knowing Yourself and Chapter 2: Knowing What You Want. We showed you how to be discerning during your phone interviews and whether your dating prospects got the green light go ahead to move forward to a face-to-face meeting or the red light where you thanked them for their time and kindly let them go. We also shared with you the logistics of how to set-up your first face-to-face encounter at a local coffee house or juice place, and how to weave into your conversation important discerning questions to discover what the person values and believes in most. And finally, we discussed how to continue the journey up this relationship mountain with your love prospect while staying focused on the evaluation process by continuing the questions and observations of your possible soulmate. Oh, and remember, this is a commitment to the long-term goal of finding your Mr. or Mrs. Right, so don't rush to jump in bed or even meet the family and friends until you've give this discerning process time to run its course. Remember, if this is the right one for you, that person will honor you and be patient just as you are being patient with him or her. So keep a plethora of notes, stay organized, and enjoy the process!

Action Plan:

We're coming down the home stretch now to finding the love of your life. All of this work will pay off, I promise! So this chapter's action plan is to come up with five or six core value questions. These questions should match your five or six top values that you came up with in Chapter 1: Knowing Yourself. Remember to review your core value questions before each phone call and each meeting so you stay connected to what is important to you and don't get too side-tracked with how the person looks or his or her hobbies and interests.

Remember to take notes after each phone call or meeting. It's so easy to think at the time that you'll write it down later or that you'll remember because it's so memorable. Don't get lazy now! Stay present and write immediately in your notebook. The discipline that you display now will pay off very, very soon. I would not have found Jim if I hadn't taken my searching seriously. Our conversations were so long that I would take notes during our phone conversations just so I wouldn't forget.

Bonus Action Plan:

For you really eager beavers out there, go the extra mile with an added review page. Track you're conversations and meetings by preparing a review page that includes the following information:

1. Appearance

2. Personality/State of Mind

3. Conversation

4. Engaged

5. Your Core Question #1

6. Your Core Question #2

7. Your Core Question #3

8. Your Core Question #4

9. Your Core Question #5

10. Next Step

Super-Tech Bonus Action Plan:

If you're a techie-type person and are familiar with CRMs (customer relationship management programs), you can set up a free mobile program to maximize your organization process. Jim and I use Zoho.com. It has a free version you can customize to your needs and meeting questions. Each love lead can be put into the program as a "lead," and besides customizing your lead form to standard information, you can also add comments and notes in a thread form so you can stay organized.

Summary Questions:

How do I logistically set-up my dates/interviews?

_____

_____

_____

_____

_____

_____

How do I keep myself safe while putting myself out into the world?

_____
_____
_____
_____
_____
_____
_____
_____
_____
_____
_____
_____
_____

How do I discern whom to continue to see versus whom to let go?

_____
_____
_____
_____
_____
_____
_____
_____
_____
_____
_____
_____
_____

What are my core value questions, and how do I use them in my choosing process?

_____
_____
_____
_____
_____
_____
_____
_____
_____
_____
_____
_____

How do I keep track of all of these suitors so I don't lose the good ones but get rid of the wrong ones?

_____
_____
_____
_____
_____
_____
_____
_____
_____
_____
_____
_____
_____

Luvaluation & Assessment List

Appearance:

Personality:

Conversation:

Core Question: _____

Core Question: _____

Core Question: _____

Core Question: _____

Core Question: _____

Next Step:

For your complimentary pdf copy of this Luvaluation/Assessment Tool, visit this url http://www.luvatlast.com/luvaluation-tools.htm or scan the following QR code:

CHAPTER 6

Finding Love in the Workplace

*"It is an extra dividend when you like the
girl you've fallen in love with."*

— Clark Gable

Before you jump into a relationship at the office with someone because he or she looks cute, take a deep breath or a cold shower and think about the benefits to consequences ratio.

- ❤ This chapter will answer the following questions:
- ❤ If I like someone in the office, should I pursue him or her?
- ❤ What should I look for in an office romance?
- ❤ What consequences should I be aware of if I pursue an office relationship?

❤ Should I tell someone that I am having a relationship at work, or should I keep it our secret?

We've discussed whom you have to be in Chapter 1 in order to describe who is right for you in Chapter 2.

We also told you how to avoid Mr. or Mrs. Wrong and how to stay focused on attracting your soulmate in Chapter 3.

Chapter 4 gave you ideas about where to find your love at last while still focusing on knowing that you'll attract more and better romantic prospects if you put your faith in the RAS.

Now we are going to address the number one place most people look for their sweethearts: the workplace. Whether it's within the confines of a large office at a mega-company or it's within a brick-and-mortar storefront, people love to pursue a love interest in the workplace.

We've all done it or at least know someone who's done it. Maybe it's because we look for reasons to goof-off in the workplace and find diversions from doing our job. Or maybe it's because it's like fishing in a crowded small pond that makes it easy and attractive to do. Whichever it is, it needs to be addressed. So the choice is once again yours!

U.S. companies spent over $208 million in the past five years in fines to the Equal Employment Opportunity Commission for sexual harassment charges. Those fines do not even begin to touch the loss in production, wages, jobs, and personal dignity when an office romance has gone wrong.

Some organizations frown upon office romances, and some may outright warn you against them. But when Cupid's arrow hits, it's hard to think about rules and office objectives because it's all about love!

And this doesn't apply to just offices; it's also small business owners, business colleagues, and any other situation where two people find themselves attracted to each other in an inappropriate work situation.

Because we are vibrant, passionate beings, we sometimes make emotional decisions that don't really fill our practical needs completely and wish we could have a "do over." But once in that situation, you can't just jump into your time machine and travel back to that moment when you made that unsuitable decision to make your workplace your romantic lair. So consider this chapter your forewarning about office dating.

Rather than tell you what to do, I'll share with you my Ten Pros and Cons of Office Dating so you get a clear understanding of the positive and negative aspects of workplace romance. So here it is, office dating, Si or No?

The Five Pros of Office Dating:

1. **It's easy access to many available romantic prospects.** Who really wants to put themselves out there in the dating world when the right person may be right there in front of you eight hours of the day? It's like ordering in your soul mate. Even if dating in the workplace is prohibited in your situation, you can't help but look and wonder whether it is worth the risk.

   As an interesting sidenote, when Jim and I were enjoying a late afternoon snack and Margarita at a local Mexican restaurant, I was so excited about writing this chapter's topic that my voice's volume kept rising to the point that the table opposite us couldn't help but eavesdrop on our conversation. I must have hit a nerve because the young lady at the next table started to turn a bright shade of red and her older man "date" hurried up to pay the check. My husband and I just looked at each other and started to giggle as he said, "I guess office dating really is more prevalent than you would think!"

2. **You get to know your love prospect without committing to a full-blown relationship.** Something can be said about getting to know someone without the pressure of a romance tied into it. You get to learn about the person in a relaxed setting that's focused on work, not on each other.

3. **You get to experience your love prospect's true characteristics right away.** The person won't feel like he or she is being evaluated, like he or she might feel if you were both dating. What better way to experience who the person is and what his or her values and beliefs are than in a neutral work setting?

My husband Jim's restaurant was a hot bed of hook-ups, one-night stands, long-term dating, and even marriages—all starting in his workplace.

One couple met while working at his restaurant. They never dated for the first year they worked together, but they slowly got to know each other during that time. Because they didn't pursue the relationship but developed the friendship, they had the opportunity to get to know each other really well without the usual pressures of formal dating.

Eventually, the male employee left the restaurant to pursue other job opportunities, and only then did he began to pursue his now wife after they really got to know each other very well.

4. **It feels safe!** Many women and men comment that the work environment gives them a feeling of safety when looking for that special person. After all, your HR department usually does a good job of weeding out the psychos and serial killers, so now all you have to do is see whether the person will match your Love by Design™ makeup.

You know I was half-joking about your company's Human Resources department weeding out the bad apples. But here is the truth about what really goes on in the hiring process that could be an advantage in your love search.

Many organizations hire a certain type of person who will fit nicely into the culture of your organization, company, or store. You're also a part of that culture, so that may give you a leg up on your love search because the people hired will be more like you than the general public.

Two good friends of mine met in one of those high-tech companies in Silicon Valley. They weren't really high on dating each other. In fact, they barely worked up a friendship at first. But the security and familiarity they experienced working in the same department year in and year out brought them closer together. Because they had a similar interest in the department they worked in, they had a common bond that expanded and grew into a real romance over time.

To this day, they admit they never would have formed a romance if it weren't for the safety of their workplace, the commonality of the work they did, and the very gradual growth of their friendship first.

They both still work for the same company, but they have a different focus in work. They even commute to work together. They don't remember what it was like before their relationship, but thank God that it happened the way it did.

5. **Love in the workplace creates an air of excitement!** People love distractions from the day-to-day routine of work and life. When they think they are a part of something new, it's exciting. It's even more exciting when it's a part of the rumor mill; like a good tabloid story, the speculation keeps the office abuzz with wonderment. Of course, this type of behavior can lead to

negative attributes, but for the most part, an innocent office romance puts a skip in anyone's step.

And if the truth comes out about you and that someone special in accounting, shipping, sales, well, your workmates can be a source of support for you, much like a family who cares about your feelings and welfare. So it can be a very positive experience in this light.

One of my friends met her husband in this way. Everyone in her department was happy for her and lived vicariously through her budding romance. What made it work well with this couple was that she worked in the office part of the business and he was in shipping and receiving. Even though their paycheck came from the same place, they rarely saw or interacted with each other during the workday. Management signed off on their relationship because it projected itself as a positive influence without any forecast of being problematic.

Now that I have shared with you the pros of dating colleagues in the workplace, let's look at…

The Five Cons of Office Dating:

1. **Post breakup!** What can start off so beautifully can end up being very, very ugly! I hope you've paid attention to the previous chapters and have done your homework. That will help prevent an office dating mistake, but you still have to prepare for the possibility that your office romance will not work out. Some breakups end up so badly that one or both of the participants in an office romance ends up leaving the department, location, or even the company.

    This exact situation happened to my friend who thought the new guy was cute. When he caught wind of her feelings, he asked her out. Their first month dating was one of infatuated bliss, but then he grew tired of her. Immediately, the temperature in the office went from hot to frigid! Production dropped off, people started to take sides (see #2 below), and eventually, they both left their jobs. Not the fantasy ending this couple was hoping for.

2. **Inter and intra-office dating can create a rift between your work groups.** Remember how the magic of romance filled the air when you began your amorous affair? How the office came together to support and encourage both of you? Now it's like an ugly divorce! With people feeling like they have to pick sides and blame the other for causing this breakup in the first place. Bad feelings can carry throughout the office, department, or store faster than a Santa Ana wind-fanned wildfire!

3. **Your situation becomes too unbearable for you to stay in your job or it becomes unbearable to your coworkers, causing you to be fired!** Most people don't like conflict of any kind. When an office romance first goes public, then goes sour, it's going to cause hurt feelings with people in the office, even if they were not part of the romance! The energy caused by the breakup can create such a strong feeling of conflict that it disrupts your life and your ability to work; ultimately, it can cause you to want to quit or it forces your boss to let you go. Not a good way to leave any workplace.

4. **Any breakup could instigate legal action.** This is especially true if one of the two former love birds was a manager, supervisor, or in some other higher level position. This situation can brings lawyers and your company into the mix, and it could become very, very ugly, especially if it's shown that the subordinate was unfairly treated after the breakup or if the rest of the work team was unfairly treated during this tryst. It could get very, very ugly!

My girlfriend worked in a very large insurance company that experienced a scandal of this sort. Her coworker was continually pursued by her supervisor to the point that she had to leave the job. Fortunately for her, this harassment was reported and documented with official office video that showed her continually rejecting his advances. He got fired, the company got sued, and she got a huge settlement, but it all could have been avoided if her supervisor had thought about the potential consequences of his behavior.

5. **It could still get ugly, even if the relationship works!** It could especially get ugly if the relationship is between a manager, owner, or any other person in a leadership role and a subordinate. Your relationship may seem like heaven to you, but it's hell for the rest of the staff. Your tryst may create jealousy, whether or not it's warranted. And even if you don't break up, you may still have the lawyers and your company all over the situation if there are complaints.

I had a friend who was a partner in and the executive chef of a very high-end restaurant in Silicon Valley during the '80s and '90s. His partner went through a very painful divorce from his wife, and when he finally emerged as ready to date again, he picked an employee from his own restaurant with whom to begin his new life of romance. To make it even more uncomfortable, this new love interest was the direct assistant to my friend. Not a very good situation at all.

At first, everything was okay with the restaurant staff. After all, they all saw how much their boss had suffered emotionally during his painful marriage breakup; it was nice to see him with a big smile on his face. I guess my friend's business partner was a bit gun shy about getting back into the dating game after so many years, so he saw this employee as an easy rebound lover.

Soon things started to change in the restaurant. What was previously a harmonious, smooth-running operation became a power struggle for culinary control. As much as my friend loved the restaurant, the workers, and the patrons, he seriously contemplated leaving along with the rest of the crew. Fortunately, it never reached that point and the romance eventually wore off. The obvious loser within this restaurant romance became my friend's assistant, and a severe breach of trust occurred between the owner and the rest of the staff. My friend's assistant soon left the restaurant because of the emotional toll it had taken on her. And that was too bad because up until this turmoil, she was a model worker and a positive asset to the kitchen team. This experience put a permanent rift between my friend and his partner. The action broke the bond of trust between them and became the beginning of the end to their working relationship together. Was acting upon a flirting impulse caused by a temporary feeling of loneliness really worth the impact it had on the many individuals within the organization?

Summary:

If you're interested in someone in your office and thinking about having an office romance—Don't Do It!

As the saying goes, there are many fish in the sea. Don't feel like you are relegated to dating the people you see every day. I understand the comfort level because of familiarity, but just don't do it.

If you are following this book's process and you're doing your homework, you'll attract your love at last anywhere in the world. But if it happens—meaning that of all the places you could possibly meet your Mr. or Mrs. Right, it just happens to be in your office, facility, or store—here is what you do: GO SLOW!

Don't act upon this impulse like you would outside of the workplace. Use this opportunity to create a friend in your potential soulmate. If this person really matches what you wrote in your manifestation letter, then go for it, but go very slow. Use the workplace as a safe zone for getting to know your coworker as a person. Learn to be a friend, learn more about the person, and do what I say: Take it slow. Have confidence in the work you put into first understanding you, and then Love by Design™, so you do not sabotage this opportunity. If this person is the right one, he will feel it too, and he will wait for the right moment.

This waiting time will also give you time to find out what are the rules to dating in your workplace. Many workplaces require that both of you declare your relationship and intentions to the Human Resources department by signing a paper that does not hold your organization responsible if a breakup occurs in the future. This also puts you on notice if you are a manager or supervisor over the department, store, or division that your love interest is also in so that everything is transparent. You may have to agree upon what happens in the case of a breakup. What actions are then taken to secure the smooth operation of your organization? Does one person need to leave or transfer to make this happen? These are the situations and issues that come about within an office romance.

Some organizations may make you transfer to a different department, store, or division once you begin your romance. So be aware of the rules before you make that step. If this person is truly the one, then leaving a job or position is nothing compared to finding your love at last. But be prepared first. You don't want any unwanted surprises at the beginning of your new relationship.

And a final word to entrepreneurs and small business owners: You may think you are immune to the scenarios I just described. But you actually may be more susceptible than you think. Even though you don't have a big office or an office at all, you work with other colleagues, vendors, and customers. Your credibility can be hurt, and your reputation can be damaged beyond repair, all because of one inappropriate transgression! Only after you've gone through the steps in this book should you approach one of your business colleagues, vendors, or customers in a romantic fashion. Maybe you won't get fired or become the scorn of the office, but you could lose your reputation and many dollars of goodwill.

Remember, the workplace is just another place for you to attract your love at last. Some studies do show that compared to other ways of meeting your future mate, meeting your love at work ranks the highest, but the people in those studies don't know what you know now. And they never had this process that you have. So ignore those studies and rest easy. Your soulmate is out there, ready to walk hand-in-hand with you on your favorite beach. But he or she doesn't need to be in the next cubicle for you to experience that!

Summary Questions:

If I like someone in the office, should I pursue him or her?

_____

_____

_____

_____

_____

_____

_____

_____

_____

_____

What should I look for in an office romance?

_____
_____
_____
_____
_____
_____
_____
_____
_____
_____
_____
_____

What consequences should I be aware of if I pursue an office relationship?

_____
_____
_____
_____
_____
_____
_____
_____
_____
_____
_____
_____
_____
_____
_____

Should I tell someone I am having a relationship at work, or should I keep it our secret?

_____

_____

_____

_____

_____

_____

_____

_____

_____

_____

_____

CHAPTER 7

Finding Your Love at Last

A man was walking on the beach one day and he found a bottle half buried in the sand. He decided to open it. Inside was a genie. The genie said, "I will grant you three wishes and three wishes only."

The man thought about his first wish and decided, "I think I want one million dollars transferred to a Swiss bank account." POOF!

Next he wished for a red sports car. POOF! There was the car sitting in front of him.

He asked for his final wish, "I wish I was irresistible to women." POOF! He turned into a box of chocolates.

— Author Unknown

This final chapter wraps up your search for Mr. or Mrs. Right in one pretty bow. In it, I will talk about how to protect yourself when you potentially meet up with not just Mr. or Mrs. Wrong but with Mr. or Mrs. Nut Job! I will also outline how to present yourself to a new prospect and dress to impress. I will show you how to entertain at home, without any cooking or entertaining experience, which would impress even the Martha Stewart types in your life. And lastly, if you feel you lost your mojo and need to get your sexy back, I have an exercise that will boost your confidence and build your sexy back quickly.

Peter: We're near the end now, Renée, so let's get right into the ways to prevent something going very wrong during your search for love at last. I assume that whether it's 2,874 or 150 love prospects, people will probably meet a few nut jobs along the way. You said that now you can get a Google voicemail so they can't stalk you. But I'm sure there are nut jobs wherever you go, so what is your advice for protecting yourself from those people? And how do you recognize whether someone is a nut job?

Renée: Women have a tendency to be more intuitive; they have what I call a spider sense where they just feel when something is wrong. I guess men feel it too since the hair on their arms or on the backs of their necks goes up. But if you're very connected to yourself, you're aware of what's going on around you and your surroundings. You need to be present with, listen to, and be watchful of someone.

That's why I tell people that when you're interviewing or dating, and you're in that kind of space, you should keep your mind clear so you don't have to think, *I didn't really feel that guy, so I have to go out with him again to be fair to him.*

People have to set aside the time in their schedules to figure out what to wear, to get dressed, maybe to put their makeup on, so it's a big deal, especially if they're entrepreneurs, not to waste time by not being present and paying attention to your dating experiences.

Peter: You're talking about connecting. Patricia's pet name for me is "freak," but there's a difference between being a freak and a nut job.

One thing you mentioned is to have Google voicemail for the phone. And secondly, you talked about going to Starbucks because you'd probably want to meet in a public place.

Renée: Starbucks, Jamba Juice—any very public place. Don't go to lunch where you're going to sit down for a couple of hours and eat because that's too much time. So coffee or Jamba Juice is where it's at.

That being said, not everybody fits into that category. I met a lot of multimillionaires when I was on Match.com. They'd read my profile and say, "I'll meet you at the Bistro Gardens," or "Let's meet at Spago's in Beverly Hills, or the Balboa Bay Club in Newport Beach. Does that sound better? I really don't like Starbucks, and you sound like a person who likes fine dining."

If that person sounds good and you think you might have a good time, get him or her on the phone and set a lunch date.

Peter: But you should do that screening on the phone prior to that; otherwise, the person kind of controls the environment and you're stuck.

Renée: That's exactly right. You don't want to be in that environment, especially if the person is going to hog the entire conversation and make it about him- or herself for three or four hours.

You want to have a back-and-forth conversation, so that's why it's important to get those people on the phone right away. If they sound like they have potential—and if you want to spend three or four hours with them at the Balboa Bay Club, Spago's, or wherever for lunch, then go and have a good time.

Peter: You also talked about having drinks with them. After the phone screening, is a public place okay to go have cocktails?

Renée: I'd rather meet them at Starbucks because there's better lighting and it's safer. If something obnoxious bugs you about the guy like dirty fingernails, or hair growing out of his ears or his nose, you can see that too in the light at Starbucks. Also with respect to safety, the Starbucks stores I go to are very busy, and for safety, the more the merrier. Back in the day, I would only give out my voicemail phone number. (There were no Google phone numbers then.) Today, I definitely would use the Google phone numbers for your interview process as well as your email process. Devote new resources just to the process of finding Mr. or Mrs. Right. So sign up for a new Google email address. Each new account has the ability to have its own phone number that your love prospects can dial to from their own phones, and then you can have their calls forwarded to your cellphone or voicemail. So if someone is trying to call you, you can have it dial right to your mobile phone. Now be aware not to call back on your cellphone unless you have the capability to block the outgoing number so it's not visible to the receiver.

Also, while we are on the subject of safety, here are a few other hints and tips to share. Never, never, never have your date pick you up at your home until you've okayed the person after the fifth date. Always meet your prospect at your meeting place. Valet park or be dropped off by a cab or Uber so you're not walking on the street to a dark parking lot late at night. Keep a small spray bottle of pepper spray on you. If you're walking in an unfamiliar area, keep the pepper spray in your hand so if you need it, it's ready to use. Also, don't meet for cocktails at the first in-person meeting. It may be fun, but remember, safety first. Besides, alcohol impairs your senses, and during this time, you want your awareness to be at its best. There will be time for cocktails once you've gotten together a few times; then it becomes appropriate.

Peter: A rule of thumb I've learned from you is that by following your process, you're screening out the nut jobs on the phone call, not during the in-person visit.

Renée: Exactly. By pre-screening through visiting the person's profile page, then evaluating his or her email message and lastly your phone conversation, you can usually spot the red flags, and if there are any, never go forward with a face-to-face meeting.

Peter: So if you did it right, unless the person throws you a curve ball out of left field that you didn't foresee coming as a sign that he or she is a nut job, you're definitely interested in the person you're meeting in a public place.

Renée: That's a good possibility. If you're frequently meeting someone in-person at Starbucks, tons of things can be answered. For example, one of your beliefs might be you really like it when somebody's on time. But if this guy is twenty minutes late and you've got another meet-up booked right behind him, you might say, "I've got a few other appointments. Would you please be on time?" You could tell whether the person has a chip on his shoulder if he responds, "What do you mean you're meeting a bunch of other people?"

Peter: You could just say, "Yeah, I've got five guys behind you. C'mon man; you're on the clock."

Renée: "Time's ticking!" But seriously, we're all adults here. This is just a first meeting, not an engagement party! I would be honest and tell the person that I am interviewing a few other guys, but I wouldn't keep repeating that fact. I'm not going to rub that in, especially since many guys have fragile egos and I'm not here to hurt someone emotionally.

Peter: That makes a lot of sense. Here's another tip for people reading this book. Let's say you went through the phone call, you're interested in the person, and then you meet face-to-face. Obviously, you want to be authentic and genuine. But you start realizing five minutes into the conversation that this person isn't the one—there are too many red flags.

How do you excuse yourself from that date, without offending the person but still remaining authentic?

Renée: As I said earlier, you can have an alarm go off on your phone. You tell the person ahead of time, "I'm waiting for an important phone call from a client, so I've possibly got an appointment." Then either have someone call you, or have the alarm go off in that twenty-two to twenty-four-minute period.

Peter: You give everybody a fair shake of thirty minutes, even if five minutes in you're still lukewarm?

Renée: Yes. You have to respect the fact that he took the time to drive to Starbucks. He's still a human being, even though he may act like a gorilla (my apologies to all of those well-groomed gorillas!). But yes, you can politely excuse yourself after giving it thirty minutes with the person. Remember, you've pre-approved this person from studying his profile, email, and talking to him over the phone, so the majority of the possible candidates that you meet up with will probably be very acceptable and, in general, good people to be around for a coffee or tea.

Peter: Now we're going to talk about how people dress. I used to think this was a big thing just for women, which I'm sure it is, about how to dress on a first date. I still get from Patricia, "You're not serious. I'm not going out of the house if you're wearing that," so she's helping me get better with all that kind of stuff. I just wear T-shirts and she says, "You can't wear that if you're going to be with me."

Going back to this first dinner date, how should you dress, and what's appropriate?

Renée: First, let's talk about when you meet at a Starbucks or Jamba Juice for the first time. I am a firm believer in first impressions, for both men and women, so I would suggest that you wear business casual. Wear what would be considered business attire in your area. In the Los Angeles area, business casual for men would be: slacks, a collared shirt, and matching shoes—a sports coat or jacket is optional. For a lady, a pant suit or skirt and blouse, appropriate accessories, and open toe shoes or pumps with a medium heel. Be aware of how much perfume or aftershave you use. Too much can be off-putting and give you the opposite results you're looking for. Don't wear workout attire, even if you've got a great body. Don't wear anything that says, "Hey, I was just in the neighborhood and thought I'd drop by...." Give the same respect to the person you're meeting as you would expect.

If it's dinner, it's going to be at a nice restaurant. A girl should wear something flattering and provocative but not slutty. I suggest the ever-popular little black cocktail dress, pearls, earrings, a necklace, black pumps, and black stockings. This is a classic look for a reason—because it works!

For guys, there's nothing wrong with jeans and T-shirts, especially for guys in Southern California. But throw on a dark blue sport coat to finish the look, which looks really handsome on a guy. A classic international look for a guy is dark gray slacks, a dark blue blazer, a white collared shirt, a handkerchief, a black belt (alligator would be stunning), and black loafers (Gucci is my fav on a guy). You could wear a dress shirt, jeans, and loafers, which is very cool too.

Peter: Oh, you like loafers? Do you hear that, Patricia? Loafers!

Patricia: Ugh, not your loafers. You have old man loafers.

Peter: No, I don't. I have nice loafers.

Renée: Not like old and overly worn loafers; something really nice. As long as they're not white.

Peter: They're not Pat Boone white. They're brown.

Anyway, Renée, you gave some advice for guys. But it seems like it's a big deal for women about how they dress, the shoes they wear, and things like that. What's some additional advice for women on a first date?

Renée: Always have your toenails done.

Peter: Why is that?

Renée: If you're wearing beautiful sandals or stilettos, it's not cool if the polish is chipped on your toenails. A lot of guys think that if the woman doesn't have her toenails manicured, she's not taking care of her hygiene and the rest of her body.

Peter: She's too "granola" for them.

Renée: Or there's too much hair underneath her makeup. Just use common sense and be watchful. Or just don't wear any nail polish at all.

Peter: If you're wearing a skirt, is there such a thing as too long or too short? And what about boom-boom shorts?

Renée: Here's how I feel about shorts and short dresses: I think they're cute and adorable, especially if you've got the legs and you can wear stilettos to show them off. But on the other hand, there's a fine line if you're going to be meeting his parents or going to church.

Peter: We're talking about the first dinner date.

Renée: You don't want to put on airs that you want to have sex on the first or second date, which isn't a good idea in general. Hold off a little bit. There are too many women who would jump into bed in a New York second because they're desperate, so I always say hold off.

Like I said earlier, once a woman gives herself physically and intimately to a man, it's harder for her to let go of him emotionally. He may be just a little bumblebee going from one flower to the next to the next, but you don't want to be another one of those flowers. It's far too common, and it's unnecessary. You want to be with a man who values you.

Like you said earlier, Peter, a lot of guys like to conquer and pursue, so hold off a little bit. Just be who you are as a woman; you don't have to put out right away because it's not necessary. The guy will hang around, but if he doesn't hang around...next! He's not a contender, so why bother? He's just going to walk out of your life anyway after he's had sex.

Peter: So that's something you want to think about.

Renée: You're a guy—you know.

Peter: But I think it works both ways for men and women because I've met some aggressive women.

Renée: There are aggressive women, and everybody's different.

Peter: Everybody thinks that guys are just going to go "Bring it on!" but that's largely a stereotype.

Renée: If women are really aggressive toward men for sex, is that a turn-on or a turn-off? Are you just going to have sex and leave her later on?

Peter: For me, personally, it's a turn-off if the woman is being very aggressive for sex. You're not looking to jump in the sack and have a one-night stand if you're looking for your ideal mate. From a guy's perspective, if you're looking to have a relationship, you want to get to know the woman just as much as she wants to get to know you and talk about things.

Renée: Getting to know each other can take it from sex to love-making when you do become intimate. Sex is just sex without the emotion, but lovemaking has emotion. Not necessarily being in love at first, but you start falling in love.

Peter: That's very true, and I'd make that same distinction. In love-making, there's an emotional connection with that person instead of "Let's just have sex."

Renée: Sex is just gymnastics in the bed. There are people who can do it for hours or days at a time, but I'm not like that because I have other things to do. Some other people don't play golf or tennis, or they don't like walks on the beach. They just like marathon sex, and that's their deal.

In the movie *Fifty Shades of Grey*, it's like, "Really? You have to use all these whips and chains and all this stuff?" I have an opinion about that too. You want to hear about that?

Peter: I certainly do since we're talking about it.

Renée: Have you ever noticed that people who are into S&M generally have a higher education level and income bracket. I've done studies on this. Because of these people's life experiences, they can't get excited with just the basic, standard sex that would excite most red-blooded Americans.

Peter: They need more stimulation, so they go out into the nether reaches of S&M.

Renée: Or whatever it is. It doesn't have to be S&M; it can be all kinds of toys. But it's different distractions. It isn't like two people who showered together and it was beautiful.

Peter: Showered? That's a biggie for you. "Let's take a shower. We're going to make love today."

Renée: If a guy only takes a shower once a week, I hit the Delete button. I don't even want to go there. I have definite rules, so if a guy takes a shower twice a day, it's like "Yay! Ding-ding-ding!"

Peter: That's a big green flag.

Renée: But once a week is a deal breaker. Cleanliness is only a belief, but my values are up there.

Peter: One last topic is how do you handle home entertaining? I'd always be concerned about ordering the wrong food or ordering in. Patricia knows I'm an old romantic.

Patricia: Mostly old.

Peter: But, Renée, you can cook up a storm and do a multi-course meal. What's your advice on handling the home entertaining aspect for a regular person?

Renée: Both of us can do that blindfolded. Are the two of you having a romantic dinner?

Peter: Let's say I feel like this woman is the right one and I really want to impress her. So I'm going to invite her into my home and make a nice home-cooked meal. But I'm beginning to get sweaty palms because I've never cooked a nice multi-course home-cooked meal. How do I go about it?

Renée: First you ask her, "Would you like to come over for dinner on Saturday night at seven? Does that sound good?" She says, "Oh that sounds great!" Because you've already taken her out seven or eight times, you'd probably know whether she drinks champagne or wine.

You might even ask her, "Are you allergic to anything?" Some people are allergic to shellfish. You might have been so mesmerized by her that every time you've taken her out to dinner, you didn't notice that she always ordered chicken or steak. She may say, "Yes, I'm allergic to shrimp," so be aware of that. Nothing kills a romantic date more than a trip to the ER!

Have the housekeeper clean the house. Or if it's already clean, great.

Have flowers on the table, and have the table set before she gets there. Often, to cut down the stress of doing last minute entertaining preparation, I'll have the table already set the day before. Try it; you'll like it too.

You don't want to have someone coming over to your house where you're pulling things out of a brown paper bag. That is the worst! So you want to create an atmosphere of "Welcome. I'm so happy you're here," without saying it verbally.

The non-verbal is having flowers on the table, the table set with a nice tablecloth, silverware, beautiful napkins and glassware, and music is playing. Have something either baking in the oven, or put some rosemary, butter, and garlic in a pan and wave it in front of the front door so she knows you've been cooking all day (even if you haven't, which is okay).

You do this at 6:50, so when she comes in at 7:00 p.m., there's a nice aroma in the house and she smells the garlic, rosemary, butter, and olive oil. Then she'll say, "Oh, wow! You've been working really hard, Peter. What a nice thing to do. I feel so blessed that you invited me to your beautiful home."

Let's say she likes chicken. If you don't know how to cook, go to Costco and buy the cooked rotisserie chicken; it's delicious. In the refrigerator section, there's tons of stuff like precooked manicotti (the noodle stuffed with meat and tomato sauce) or mashed potatoes. Follow the directions, put it in the oven, take it out of that stupid plastic thing, and throw it away.

Peter: For God's sake don't have it in the metal tin. Put it in a baking dish.

Renée: Have it already done, put it in a serving dish, and cover it with plastic wrap. Get rid of all the evidence (the cover and the container the chicken came in) so you don't get caught.

There are even pre-made salads at Costco, where they include everything you need to make a delicious salad course. Wash the lettuce in Kangen water, even if it says it's pre-washed, and dry it well in a colander or salad spinner if you have one. The dressing is already made and stored in the package, and there are nuts, cranberries, and toppings. Just put it all in a bowl, toss it all together, and have it on the table. It's not a big deal.

Have a pie or pound cake already done. Don't have it in the package. Slice it and put it on a platter.

It takes only forty-five minutes to get all this stuff done. But you've got to put all the containers in the garbage can, take the trash outside, and put a new liner in the trashcan.

Peter: So the evidence is gone.

Renée: You've got to get rid of the evidence. Even if they find out later that you can't really cook, that's okay because you get a big "A" for effort, and it shows that you know how to entertain and make the other person feel special. And that's the bottom line—to make your date feel like he or she deserves a pampered experience put on by you.

If this is the tenth or twelfth date, and you think this could be the night of your first "encounter," make sure the housekeeper was there that day or the day before and the bathroom is clean. Make sure your sheets are clean, you have candles on the nightstands, and condoms are on your bedside ready to go.

Peter: Got it.

Renée: That's basic stuff. Some guys forget that, and they haven't washed their sheets in months. Then the woman will think, *Hello? Are you kidding me?* That never happened to me because the people I slept with always had housekeepers. But I'm talking about regular single guys who haven't been "housebroken" yet.

Just make sure your sheets are clean, the rugs are vacuumed, the bathroom's spotless, and extra guest towels are there just in case. I don't believe in that, "Accept me the way I am" bullsh*t! It's a sign of respect when you go the extra mile to make your guest feel welcome. How you live on your own is your own business, but step it up when you are entertaining a guest who just might become your Mr. or Mrs. Right!

Peter: I want to get back to the olfactory senses because people's odors can really turn people off. We've learned in neuroscience that the Croc Brain goes past your filtering mechanism right into your limbic system, so odors are very important.

You said to light candles. But are there scented candles you should have, and some that are definite no-nos that would probably turn somebody off?

Renée: Candles are nice. You want to go higher end, especially if you live near a Nordstrom where they sell nicer candles than at a drugstore.

Peter: No Big Lots stores?

Renée: No Big Lots, unless you're already married; then that's fine. But if you want to impress somebody, definitely have something with a pretty fragrance. Ask the salesperson at the store which scents are more popular for promoting romance. Some of the popular smells are cinnamon, pumpkin (the pumpkin pie smell is always a hit), vanilla (remember Granny from *The Beverly Hillbillies* would tell Elly May, "A dash of vanilla behind your ears drives men wild!"), lavender, orange (Jim loves this smell), and jasmine.

Nordstrom or Neiman Marcus sells nice candles for around $30. I know that's on the high end, but their aroma fills the entire house really fast, and you get what you pay for. This person may be the one, so go for it. You can get candles without a fragrance, but you can get those at Big Lots or a drugstore. At least have the house decorated, and nice smells going on. Remember, it's all about creating an atmosphere that is conducive to making your guest feel special, relaxed, and romantic.

Peter: The theme I'm hearing is if the atmosphere is excellent, the food can be kind of mediocre and you'll still be okay.

Renée: The food doesn't have to be mediocre because many good grocery stores have some really good, freshly prepared, pre-made dinners that are very tasty besides being convenient. But it's all about the presentation. If you're presenting something out of a plastic Costco container—and she got all dressed up for a $5.00 Costco chicken—I don't think so.

But if you present it where you take the string off the chicken, you cut the chicken up a little bit, and you put a little garnish in like parsley and throw some vegetables around it, you've at least made an attempt to make it look good. Today's grocery markets have so many ready-to-heat-and-eat foods that it doesn't take much effort to entertain well at home. In fact, if you're a total basket case in the kitchen and can't even come up with a plan, go to an upscale market or a good friendly market that has helpful people ready to assist you. Visit the store in the afternoon when it's a bit slower so you'll have these people's full attention. Tell them you're entertaining the possible Mr. or Mrs. Right, but you have no idea what to serve. I guarantee they will take care of you and make your dinner party a big hit.

Peter: We've been doing a lot of kidding, but in all seriousness, I think you're right. It doesn't have to be home-cooked, but it should show that you put your heart into it. The woman or man will pick up on the little things you do, and that really matters.

Renée: Bottom line is if you put the Costco chicken on the table in a plastic container, and the potatoes are coming out of the microwave, it's like, "You didn't really try, so why should I have sex with you? This is really stupid. You're a big-time partner in a law firm, and this is so frickin' lame." That's what's going to resonate subconsciously with her.

Whereas, if you made the effort to put it on a platter or another plate, and throw some parsley and vegetables around it—and it's hot and you put it on the table—it'll look like you put effort and love into it. You may not be in love with this woman yet, but you put the love into the dinner that you served.

If you and Patricia have been out to dinner, and there's not enough seasoning and you just don't feel the love and care in the entrée you just ordered, it's because the chef either had an argument with his wife or his girlfriend, or his wife found out about the girlfriend. You can feel it because the food isn't quite there. It's missing that special ingredient that separates good food from great—TLC (tender loving care). It's real, not just a joke. So make sure you make the effort to make your time together special because he or she will feel it.

I mentioned this earlier, but one of the most pleasurable activities a couple can do is to prepare a romantic dinner in the kitchen together (just a hint to what dessert might be). Jim and I will do that as a fun change of pace from the "day to day, let's get the food on the table because it's been a long day in the office" situation. We'll do what I've coined Date Night-In™. I teach this concept to my students who have graduated to a committed relationship or have come to me seeking help in discovering ways to spice up their love lives. Date Night-In is part of the concept for keeping that fire burning bright for each other no matter how hectic and chaotic your life may seem. But more on that after you find the love of your life.

Peter: That makes a lot of sense. Well, Renée, thank you very much for sharing all of your wisdom and advice. We've covered a lot in this book.

Renée: You're welcome, Peter. If any of my readers like what I just shared with you on creating that special Date Night In™ or they just want to know how to entertain for that special person, my next book coming out is *Garlic to Garter Belts*. It's about creating magic moments for anyone in a committed relationship who wants to keep the fire of passion burning bright between the two of them. In fact, I'll include a few easy recipes at the end of this chapter just to give you a head start for planning your next Date Night-In™.

Peter: Thanks, Renée, and remind us where we can go online if we want to follow you or watch for updates on your future books. It's LuvatLast.com, right?

Renée: Correct. You can find me at LuvatLast.com, FindingYour-LoveatLast.com, or ReneeMichelleGordon.com

Peter: And if readers want to learn more, I know you have a one-day workshop that's absolutely fantastic. You also do workshops both online and in person as well as offer a one-on-one platinum coaching package to help people personalize their searches for finding love at last. I believe this coaching program is for the person who is time challenged, has been out of the dating game for a while, and needs a bit of hand holding.

Renée: That's right, Peter. The Platinum Coaching Package works well for most of the people I help, but I also have created a package for the elite soul out there who needs more support—my in-person, one-day coaching Protégé Package.

Peter: Tell us a little about that. What's the one-day coaching Protégé Package about?

Renée: It's more of a high-end one-day coaching. It's for someone who wants to find the love of his or her life really fast without having to struggle with doing all of the work alone. I help people through the foundational self-discovery work faster so they can get to the uplifting Love by Design™ part quicker. And because I'm there in person, I can make sure they design their ideal Mr. or Mrs. Right and don't fall victim to repeating old lover patterns from the past.

I also help them with different selections in their wardrobe, and with styling what they're wearing as well as hair, makeup, etc. I could do that with a man as well (but with no makeup) by looking at his suits, his jeans, or whatever he's wearing.

I look at people's homes and tell them they can do this or that to attract the right person.

I also look at their etiquette and poise. I kind of go through the process of "Let's go on a date for a half-hour," and then I'll write notes. If he doesn't open the car door for me, I'll correct him and say, "You need to open the car door and help me out by taking my hand." We'll do this as a back-and-forth exercise for five or six times until he gets it right.

I show a woman how to get into a car without spreading her legs and showing her thong. Little things like that show the woman is poised and has etiquette and sophistication.

I'll help you accelerate your search, even if you've been alone for many years because of a bad public marital breakup or the heart-break of your first spouse passing away. I'll help you heal your wounds, focus on what will make you happy, and hold you by the hand during your search for your new love at last!

I'll even throw a security background check into your package for those people who are in the public arena—CEOs, entertainment stars, celebrities, or sports figures—who need that extra level of certainty that they are attracting the right person.

Peter: Wow, you think of everything! I can definitely see how your one-on-one coaching can really accelerate for someone the process of what this book's goal has been: Finding Your Love at Last.

Renée, I really appreciate your time and advice. I learned a lot from you, and we had some good laughs along the way as well. So thank you.

Renée: Thank you, Peter. And thank you, Patricia!

Patricia: You're welcome!

Renée: Finally, remember, you don't need to be in a relationship to be complete. You're complete because of who you are, not because of whom you're with.

Summary Questions:

What are some of the things I can do to keep myself safe from the "nut jobs" out there?

_____

_____

_____

_____

_____

_____

How can I bring my sexy back?

_____
_____
_____
_____
_____
_____
_____
_____

How can I present and dress myself for our first meet-up and first date?

_____
_____
_____
_____
_____
_____
_____

How can I entertain and impress a date at home when I can barely boil water?

_____
_____
_____
_____
_____
_____
_____

When is the right time to decide to have sex?

_____
_____
_____
_____
_____
_____
_____
_____

BONUS DATE NIGHT-IN™ RECIPES

Nothing is more attractive and appealing than having your special person make dinner for you. After you've done the restaurant date, hiking date, picnic date, movie date, party date, run in the park date, and baseball game date, and you now know this is a special person who could be the one, dinner is the next step.

You don't have to be a world class chef like my husband Jim or me, but you do need to put your love and care into the evening. I've included a few Date Night-in™ recipes to help you get started.

The main thing about an in-home romantic meal is not just how good the food is, but also how appealing the setting is and how strongly the romantic vibe is resonating. I gave you some great ideas earlier in the chapter for setting the tone, like with burning nicely scented candles, adding the aroma of rosemary and garlic in the room ten minutes before your guest's arrival, and having smooth music playing in the background.

A few other fun ideas are adding more pillows on the floor and eating dinner or at least dessert on the floor in front of the coffee table. Or having an aphrodisiac-themed meal that shows you've done a bit of research to make the evening special. Maybe even making the whole meal a silverware-less experience where you feed each other by hand! Just make sure that your dating experience has progressed to that level and you're not scaring away your love prospect by being too aggressive in your planning so that he or she gets the wrong idea.

So going back to the idea of eating the whole dinner on the floor—I think for the first time, let's plan on eating at the table first, and then having dessert on the pillow-laden floor. At least you're certain you'll get to eat this special meal together first!

We'll still use the aphrodisiac theme to add a thrill to the meal. So here are the top ten aphrodisiac foods for various reasons. According to the *Encyclopedia Britannica*, an aphrodisiac is any of various forms of stimulation thought to arouse sexual excitement. Aphrodisiacs may be classified into two principal groups:

Psycho-physiological (visual, tactile, olfactory, aural)

Internal (stemming from food, alcoholic drinks, drugs, love potions, medical preparations)

So the top ten aphrodisiac foods may be part of folklore, nutrition-based, genitalia-shaped, or traditionally known as an aphrodisiac. Whichever you believe, eating them is all about creating the moment and having fun. Here is the list:

1. Oysters, especially raw
2. Seafood in general
3. Garlic
4. Honey
5. Chocolate
6. Basil

7. Bananas

8. Avocado

9. Almonds

10. Asparagus

Here is a fun aphrodisiac menu that is easy to prepare, serve, and enjoy!

Hot & Smoky Almonds

(This is a snack to have with cocktails on arrival)

Grilled Asparagus Mimosa Salad

~

Seafood Pesto Pasta

(A light red wine like a Pinot Noir or clean, crisp chilled white like a Chenin Blanc or Champagne would be great.)

~

(Time to move over to the pillow/coffee table area.)

Spicy Chocolate Dipped Bananas Fondue with Basil

Recipes

Grilled Asparagus Mimosa

Serves 4
Prep Time 10 minutes
Cook Time 10 minutes

Ingredients:

2 whole eggs
To taste Kosher salt
2 tablespoons capers
2 bunches asparagus, pencil size or larger
2 tablespoons olive oil
1 teaspoon black pepper
1 lemon

Procedure:

Fill a 6 to 8 quart sauce pan with good clean water and add salt to taste. Add a tablespoon of distilled white vinegar to your water. Bring to a boil and add your eggs in the shell. Cook for approximately 9 minutes. Remove the eggs from the boiling water and plunge them in an ice water bath. Once eggs are slightly chilled, peel off all of the shell; then chop with a knife or grate through a large hole grater. Mix with a pinch of salt and the capers. Reserve for later.

While the eggs are boiling, prepare your asparagus to grill. If they are very large asparagus, they can be peeled. Run your peeler from the base of the asparagus tips to the base of the asparagus stalk.

Trim the asparagus stalk where it begins to be tough. A simple test is to hold one end of the asparagus in one hand and the other end of the asparagus in the other. Bend the asparagus until the tough end breaks off. Repeat that for the rest of your asparagus.

Toss your cleaned asparagus in the olive oil. Sprinkle with salt and black pepper. Heat an iron pan, stove top grill pan, or even open outdoor grill to medium high heat. Cook the asparagus on all sides to caramelize and bring out its natural sweetness. Cook until it just becomes tender. Piercing with a fork will show its doneness. Place on a serving platter and cover with the chopped egg and caper mixture and squeeze of lemon. Serve and enjoy!

Seafood Pesto Pasta

Serves 2
Prep Time 15 minutes
Cook Time 5 minutes

Ingredients:

1/2 lb. linguini or fettuccini dry pasta
6 tablespoons extra virgin olive oil
1/2 lb. seafood (shrimp, scallops) peeled
6 Manila clams
1 tablespoon chopped garlic
Pinch red pepper flakes
2 oz. dry white wine
4 oz. clam juice (bottled)
3 tablespoons basil pesto (store bought and prepared)
1/2 lemon
To taste, salt and black pepper

Procedure:

This method was created so you don't have to do too much work when you are entertaining. So you'll pre-blanch or par-cook the pasta and reserve it to the side. Then you make the pesto sauce in a pan and reserve that to the side. All you have to do is warm the sauce, toss in the pasta, adjust the seasoning, and serve.

Pre-blanch the pasta in boiling and salted water. Add 1 tablespoon of olive oil to the water and add your pasta. Cook the pasta until it's al dente or just a bit underdone. Drain into a colander and cool quickly with cold water. Toss in 1 tablespoon of extra virgin olive oil on a plate, cover with plastic wrap, and reserve to the side.

Heat a large sauce pan with 2 tablespoons of extra virgin olive oil to medium high heat. Add the chopped garlic. Sauce for 20 seconds. Meanwhile, season the peeled and deveined shrimp and scallops. Add the shrimp, scallops, and clams to the pan. Toss around for another 20 seconds. Add the white wine, red pepper flakes, and clam juice. Cover and just bring to a boil. Then turn off the heat. Reserve to the side so it's warm but not cooking. (This method can only be done if your guest will be arriving within the next 30 minutes. Otherwise, do this step in front of your guest to keep the seafood fresh and safe.)

When you are ready to serve the pasta, heat the seafood, add the pesto and the pasta, and toss together until warmed through. Finish off the heat with lemon juice, 1 tablespoon of extra virgin olive oil, and salt and black pepper to taste.

Arrange by twirling the pasta with a large fork onto the plate and arrange the clams, shrimp, and scallops attractively around the pasta. Garnish with a fresh basil leaf and serve.

I know if you're Italian, you don't serve grated parmesan with this dish. But if you're American like me, go for it; it's yummy!

Spicy Chocolate Dipped Bananas Fondue with Basil

Serves 4
Prep Time 10 minutes
Cook Time 10 minutes

Ingredients:

1 pound dark chocolate, high quality
1 cup heavy cream
1 pinch organic sea salt
1/2 tablespoon Cheyenne pepper
1 pinch chipotle pepper powder
1 shot George Dickel Tennessee Whiskey
1 bunch basil leaves, fresh only
4 bananas

Procedure:

Chop the chocolate into small pieces and place in a glass or stainless bowl. Cover with plastic wrap. Place over a double boiler over simmering water to melt the chocolate to barely half-melted.

Meanwhile, in a dry sauce pan, heat your Cheyenne pepper and chipotle powder to roast and release the flavors. Add your heavy cream, whiskey, and salt, and bring to barely a simmer. Pour over the half-melted chocolate and stir until smooth.

If you have a fondue set up, pour the melted chocolate mixture in the fondue pot and serve. This can be set up and kept warm to the side and be done in advance, or you can have fun making it together. Your choice!

Warm your honey slightly in a pot in warm water. Cut your basil leaves by first rolling them into a cigar shape, then cutting them very thin. Add this to the honey.

To serve, have your bananas peeled and cut into bite-size pieces. Alternate dipping them into the warm chocolate fondue and basil honey with special fondue forks, or if the chocolate is not too warm, use your fingers to feed each other. Then find creative ways to clean up your chocolate mess!

Special Reports

Bringing Back Your Mojo

Here are some hints and tips on being authentically sexy to bring back your mojo!

I know that for many of you, this is a huge step—putting yourself out to the world of love. You may feel a little timid and lacking confidence in your sexy self. But being sexy is a state of mind, so it's all about changing your mind. In the words of Tony Robbins, "Sometimes you've got to fake it to make it!"

So you may not be as confident as you once were in the sexy department. But here is the good news: You can train yourself to feel and be sexier. I have my list of the top twenty-nine everyday things you can do to be sexier. Pick one a day for each day of the month; then repeat your favorite one over on the last day. And in one month, you'll feel sexier, more appealing, and a ton more confident about your self-worth.

1. **Strut around the house like Mick Jagger.** You know what I'm talking about; no one acts sexier than Mick Jagger on stage. Put on your favorite strut'n music, strap on that air guitar, and prance around the house like the superstar you are! (Don't forget to exaggerate those lips like Mick!)

2. **Always make eye contact.** And not just with your partner— looking everyone you're interacting with squarely in the eye will not only boost your own confidence, but it'll get people to see you as confident and in control, which usually translates to sexiness for both men and women.

3. **You've got a brain—so use it!** But don't be a know-it-all. People admire smarts; they're akin to healthy skin, clear eyes, and healthy hair (or a healthy scalp for those who are hair-challenged). Take the day to improve your knowledge in a wide variety of subjects, current events, history, famous people, art, etc.... Be aware; a smarty pants or a corrector will have the opposite effect and make you very unsexy.

4. **Humor counts high on the sexy-meter.** You don't have to be the next Jerry Seinfeld or Ellen DeGeneres, but having a sense of humor counts. Take a day to watch the comedy channel and listen to the timing of a well-crafted joke. You don't have to have a full-on comedy routine, but if you look for what is funny in the world, you'll come across sexier to others and yourself.

5. **Smile, employ an upbeat attitude, and have expressive eyes.** Being friendly and upbeat is very sexy, so go for it! Make a concerted effort to smile at people whom you never noticed before. Give them a little smile with that "I'm too sexy for my smile" attitude. Have fun with it!

6. **Find a good tailor.** When clothes are too boxy, too long, or generally ill-fitting, it looks like you're trying to cover up your body, which intrinsically translates to being conservative or generally unsexy. No need to prance around in skin-tight numbers (except when you're doing sexy tip #1), but a well-fitting dress with a nipped waist and a flattering hemline looks sexy. Pick one piece from your wardrobe that you'll wear on one of your many dates that will make you feel sexy.

7. **Challenge yourself.** Whether it's at work or even something as small as taking an advanced fitness class instead of a beginner one, succeeding will give you an air of confidence that will travel with you, making you even sexier.

8. **Slow and easy conversation will kick up the cool/sexy look**

and feel. By slowing down your normal speech pattern just a tad, you transform yourself instantly. Also, remember the power is in the pause. When you're in a conversation and making a point, hold and pause just a second more to emphasize your point, and oooooh, so sexy! Oh, and remember that eye contact as you're doing it.

9. **Don't wear underwear on a date or first meet-up.** Go "commando" once in a while. It's totally cliché, but sometimes having a sexy secret makes you feel, and appear, sexier. Even just walking around grocery shopping, you know you've got a sexy little secret that no one else knows makes you sexy.

10. **Get a manicure and pedicure.** This means you too, guys! It's often the small indulgences that make us look and feel our best, so taking time for a professional manicure and pedicure once in a while can do wonders for your confidence.

11. **Be kind and have etiquette.** No matter what you look like, nothing will knock your innate sex appeal down faster than being rude to people. You don't need to, for lack of a better phrase, "kiss ass" and be phony, but treating everyone, including service people at a restaurant, your valet, friends, new people, and your elders with basic kindness and respect is an attractive quality.

12. **Get a spray tan.** Likewise, having a healthy glow not only makes most men and women feel sexier, but it also has a slimming effect. It's definitely a win-win.

13. **Hone your talents.** Lots (and lots) of rock stars, writers, actors, and artists aren't traditionally attractive, but there's a reason why they seem so damn sexy: Talent and Attitude. There's something primally attractive about someone with strong skills who knows it, so take time to develop whatever it is you're gifted in. But in the meantime, like Tony said earlier, "Fake it till you make it," works.

14. **Be assertive.** Wet blankets aren't sexy. If you want something that you believe you deserve, if you know you're correct, or if your date suggests going somewhere you don't want to, speak up. Being assertive is different from merely being pushy, and it happens to be a sexy and admirable quality. "Wishy-washy" can get really old, really fast.

15. **Play up your best features.** When it comes to our looks, we all have certain attributes we like better than others, so why not make them the first thing people see when they look at you? Bring the focus to your assets and act it out. If you've got great legs, then go back to the "strut." If you've got lips to rival Angelina Jolie, buy a bright gloss to accent them.

16. **Hold back a little with your conversation.** I'm not saying you have to become a full-on creature of mystery, but I'd advise against spilling personal details people don't really need to know right away, such as your parents' messy divorce, your chronic stomachaches, your huge fight with your best friend, the fact you're obsessed with planning your wedding, or that you're only meeting losers on dating sites. Keep it to yourself—a little mystery goes a long way, and as in life, like in the movies, that mystery man or woman always comes across as very, very sexy.

17. **Put your phone away or just shut it off.** This is a big one, so pay attention: The act of obsessively checking your phone every two minutes could be a definite deal breaker when it comes to sex appeal. There's nothing ruder than trying to have a conversation with a person who's constantly staring at his or her screens. Wouldn't you be put off if someone were paying more attention to his or her iPhone than to you? Being present is sexy. Being preoccupied is not.

18. **Compliment, question, question.** Compliments go a long

way. Make sure you are sincere and genuine. Your date will sense if there is a lack of integrity. On a date (or anytime you're with another human, really), it's a good bet that asking questions will always ensure flowing conversation. However, if you start grilling people on politics, religion, their exs, or how much cash they pull in, you're going to look nosy and abrasive, rather than sexy and seductive.

19. **Touch yourself.** Yeah, I'm going there. Women who masturbate know exactly what they like when they're intimate with someone else, which only increases their sex appeal. (Remember: "Be in love with yourself and honor yourself; don't sleep with anyone who doesn't value you.") I met a woman at one of the many personal development programs I've taken, who proclaimed herself to be the sexiest woman in the world. I've got to admit she did have an amazingly sexy aura about her. She literally had an orgasm in front of the class without touching herself! She told us she had developed her sense of sexiness over many years, and she could turn it on or off at any given time. She showed how sexiness was truly between the ears and could be developed. So there is hope for us all!

20. **Undo yourself a bit.** Unbutton one extra button on your blouse, smudge your eyeliner, and spritz some fragrance spray in your hair. Sometimes appearing as if you just had fun in bed can make you feel and look extra-sexy.

21. **Try new things.** Whether it's a taking a dance class, trying a new restaurant in a new neighborhood, or booking a last-minute weekend getaway, trying new things can absolutely make you feel sexier. Visualize yourself as a new adventurer and throw caution to the wind. "Novelty is the greatest aphrodisiac." Dr. Sandor Gardos, Ph.D. and international sex therapist, says that living in the moment is exciting and sexy.

22. **Be comfortable in your own skin.** As cliché as it sounds, nothing says sexy like the swagger that comes with truly being comfortable with yourself. If you're not, do something about it, whether that means joining a gym, getting a new job, moving to another city, or surrounding yourself with more supportive people. After all, complete confidence is the key component of sex appeal.

23. **Have more sex.** It might seem obvious, but the more sex you have, the sexier you'll be perceived to be for long periods of time. Through my research with Peter Lisoskie, human behavior expert, I found that oxytocin, the hormone responsible for creating feelings of love, is elevated in men after sex, and that oxytocin drives men in committed relationships to stay away from other women.

24. **Don't be a snooze-fest.** This might sound harsh, because we know you're not boring, but if people ask you questions, and you give one-word answers, roll your eyes, or seem generally disinterested, you're not doing yourself any favors. Even if you look like a supermodel, people are most turned on by stimulating conversation, eye contact, and personality.

25. **Take up yoga.** A study in the *Journal of Sexual Medicine* found that women who regularly did yoga actually felt sexier. Why? Researchers say it could be because yoga encourages a stronger mind-body connection. Also, the fact that yoga makes you be very present with yourself adds to you feeling sexier.

26. **Copy the characteristics of the sexiest people you know.** Who feels sexy to you? Think about it, and then think about what it is that they do that seems sexy. Now do the same. Copy what they do and repeat it throughout the day with different people just to get a thrill. But more importantly, act it out for you and have fun!

27. **Invest in a chic pair of sunglasses.** There's nothing like the ritual of trying on a cool pair of sunglasses to get your groove on. Spend the day striking the pose at every mirror you can find, and once again, have fun with it.

28. **Watch a sexy movie and imagine you're its star.** I watched the movie *Fifty Shades of Grey* with my husband, and I got all hot and bothered during most of the movie. It especially was powerful because I had read the books as well so I knew what was coming, and that peaked my excitement even more.

29. **Use sexy men or women to your advantage, rather than comparing yourself to them.** Instead of comparing yourself to other men or women whom you think are sexy, take cues from them. For example, stop moaning about the fact that you're not as tall, thin, or busty as a Victoria's Secret model or as smooth as George Clooney. Instead, start using to your advantage the things that you know make them sexy. This might mean taking an extra fifteen or twenty minutes in the morning to create the same bombshell waves in your hair, getting a light spray tan, or tying that perfect tie knot. There's no proof that these men or women are innately sexier than you; they just put in more effort.

Remember, ultimately, sexier starts between the ears. So the sexier you act, the more you become just that: sexier. So go for it. Have fun and let that sexy side of you come forward!

How to Write a Winning Profile

Designing Your Profile:

I didn't put this into the earlier chapter "Knowing Where to Find Mr. or Mrs. Right" because I didn't want you to be confused about what is a priority in finding your soulmate. People who haven't read this book think (as you may have thought before knowing this information) that all there is to finding Mr. or Mrs. Right is going online and posting a wanted ad. Or finding your life mate at a friend's wedding. Or my favorite: Waiting around until someone shows up at your doorstep! I mean, that's okay if you have the hots for the UPS guy!

But you now know there's a lot more required to the search, so you'll understand why I've put this part at the end of the book, not right up front or even in the middle. Because finding Mr. or Mrs. Right is all about creating the circumstances to attract that person—not advertise for that person. As I've said before, online searching for your soulmate is a very effective tool. Heck, that's how I found Jim. But you have to do the foundational work before you jump into the boiling pot of online dating.

With that being said, many of my clients have asked for help in this area. They want to do all of the groundwork so they can express themselves clearly by using this powerful search tool. What I tell them is that if you've done your homework from this book already, this part should be fairly simple.

So here are the five parts to designing your perfect profile:

1. Headline

2. Headshots and Pictures

3. Who You Are

4. What You Want

5. Contact Information

Let's look at each one in detail:

1. **Headline:** Remember, this is what got my honey to take notice of me. If you're a woman, don't ask someone to be your soulmate. It's way too soon for that. And if he responds that he will, he probably won't last. Do be a bit outrageous. Remember, it's an attention getter. This is also a good time to express who you are without saying who you are.

    I used the headline, *Ex-Model/Chef,* which was also accurate. I was a former Shiseido cosmetics model, and I am also a formally trained and experienced chef. So I was being me, but stating it in a way that made people curious. Jim liked the duality of the headline. On one hand, a model is focused on looking good all of the time, meaning she is always dieting to stay fit and look lean for the camera. While a trained chef will express herself with food and freely taste all of her creations, unconcerned about the calorie count. So this got Jim to check out who this person was and find out whether the headline was accurate.

    Have fun with your headline. Spend the most time creating it. I know from experience, in my classes, workshops, and private coaching, that we spend most of our profile-building time on this part because it's so important. When it's not you writing about you, it's so much easier to help write a profile headline. That is exactly why many people who may even read this book will opt to use my live workshop and one-on-one coaching options. If you don't currently have the resources for my workshops or coaching services, I usually suggest coming up with three or four different headlines and asking some close friends for their opinions. If you're really ambitious, get a good book on marketing headlines to gain some insight into how to write a headline in general. And if you're a real go-getter, use that information to create a couple of kick-butt headlines and test them on two different profiles about you. This is called "split testing," and it's a good way to narrow down which headline performs the best. I know this sounds like I'm teaching you marketing skills, and guess what? I am. Remember, my background is in business, and I've always said that you should remove your emotions out of the love search process and treat it more like marketing and promoting yourself. Finding your love at last is not too different from effective business marketing in the sense that you have to know your ideal client, in this case, your ideal mate; then you need to know how to communicate that you are here for him or her.

Maybe you don't want 2,874 love prospects contacting you, but you do want as many eyeballs looking at your profile as possible in the hopes that you'll snag the right one.

2. **Headshot and picture:** Spend the money to get it done right. This is an investment in your life, and you are worth it! I was fortunate to have professional photo shots already done. You may never have had any headshots taken in your life. Now is the time. Don't get too caught up with casual snapshots, pictures with pets, pictures with friends (we all know you have friends, so no need to show them off too), or worse, photos with your ex-husband, ex-wife, ex-girlfriend, ex-lover, etc.!

Here is what I recommend you don't post:

- 💜 A picture of yourself from twenty years ago, prom pictures, or any old photo just to be cute.

- 💜 A picture with your pets, kids, nieces, nephews, family, friends, etc. It's supposed to be about *you*.

- 💜 Risqué shots of certain parts of your body. Remember, this is for the love of your life, not the love for tonight!

- 💜 An avatar of yourself, even if you're into anime, roleplaying, etc.

- 💜 Pictures of you wearing sunglasses, floppy hats, or anything that hides your face.

- 💜 Someone else's picture.

No picture at all. Don't worry; if you're not physically attractive or you don't take a good photo, that's okay because you'll attract your love at last regardless. If you love yourself, it will come through in your photo and the right person will see the real you.

What you do post:

- 💜 The most recent photo of yourself.

- 💜 A photo of professional quality from someone who knows visually how to pull out your best features. No selfies!

- 💜 A headshot, full or partial body shot, and personality shots are the three types of photo shots you should focus on. Even if you carry a few extra pounds, that's okay; that is who you currently are. Love your body and the right person will love you. Full body should be standing and posed. Take multiple types of headshots from front angles and different side angles. Find a photographer who can capture your personality. If you follow someone on Facebook or other social media who has a photo that captures his or her personality, ask the person who took it. I do this with my different speaker friends. They all have decent pictures of themselves, but you always can tell when someone found the right photographer—the person who really captured the essence of who he or she is visually. That's what you want too.

❤ Capture your personality. If you're playful, show playfulness. If you're athletic, take a photo in your tennis, golf, or volleyball outfit. Be careful in this picture; you don't want to be peg-holed as a tennis player, golfer, or volleyball fanatic. Remember, these are activities that you enjoy, but if you remember from Chapter 1: Knowing Yourself, you are more than what you do. You are first your values and beliefs.

❤ Color and/or black and white is okay. Sometimes, photos taken in black and white can express more emotion than color photos. If you like black and white, make sure the photo is taken by someone who specializes in black and white stylings.

❤ If your dating profile system allows more photos, just keep repeating those three main shots of head, body, and personality. Once again, that Fourth of July picnic at Uncle Ned's may have been a fun time, but rarely does an iPhone on a stick capture your essence.

3. **Who You Are:** Use your knowledge about yourself to give someone a clear idea of who you are and the values you hold. If there is room on your profile page, include a short story to illustrate those key points. For example, if you believe in the

value of all living things, health, and family, you may have a story that sounds like this:

To understand more of who I am, during my off time, I like taking nature hikes in the local hills like I did with my nieces and nephews last spring. Besides enjoying the outdoors and exercise in general, I find that hiking gives me a chance to connect with nature and Mother Earth. In fact, in this one particular excursion, we even had a chance to rescue a baby bird who had fallen out of the nest and protect it from predators on the hunt....

You can see how even a few short sentences within a story can tell the reader more about you than a laundry list of your values and beliefs.

Remember, this is a profile that gives the reader/searcher a taste of who you are. Make it accurate enough to show you off and brief enough to make people want more. Most people are going to have a judgment about you from the headline and photo array. They will skim the profile about your personality, and if it's not off-putting, they will go right to the last part of what you want. This is where you want to separate the love prospects from the pretenders so you don't have to waste your time apologizing to them for not being their type. Just get it over with in this next part.

4. **What You Want:** Eliminate the pretenders in advance with honesty. Remember, it's not a popularity contest about how many people you can attract; it's attracting the right one! So when you write about what you want in a person, use the information that you came up with from your Love by Design™ section in Chapter 2. Because you know what is so important to you, you must be discerning in this part of the profile. If you aren't, you'll attract 2,874 potential suitors like I did, until I refined this part of my process. So be honest and to the point

about what you want. Make sure you include your "musts" in the list; if no smoking is a must, make sure it's in there. Don't be afraid to tell someone what you want. You are doing yourself and the other person a big service by being brutally honest now. People who haven't read this book find online dating so exhausting and time-consuming because they don't know what they really want and what person is right for them, according to their values and beliefs. So they are trying to find their soulmates as if they were shooting arrows at erratically moving targets.

So if you want a person over fifty years old, with children over sixteen, who is an entrepreneur, believes in God, and values family, financial freedom, and health, and takes at least two showers a day, then write it down and begin the manifestation process. Don't shortchange yourself. You deserve exactly what you want and need in life.

By the way, the description I just used in this example was posted in my profile back when I found my love at last. In fact, Jim told me he was attracted to me through my profile for my direct and clear communication about what I wanted—a real turn-on for him.

5. **Contact info:** Remember to have your Google phone number set up along with your dating Gmail account that goes with it. You want that barrier of safety between you and the unknown world of online daters.

Last words on online dating and writing a winning profile

Remember, this is not a popularity contest. This is not social media where the more friends you have, the better. This is about finding your love at last. Be very clear about that objective when you are setting up this part. It's very easy to get caught up in wanting to be the most popular person to the point where you stop being yourself and start playing to the crowd. Use this amazing Internet tool for its true purpose—to be the most efficient way to connect you to your love at last, but do your homework first! Complete the exercises provided for each chapter or work with me and my team to make sure you are grounded to who you are and who is the right person for you. It's very easy to get overwhelmed by the vast number of interesting people on any of these dating search engines. That's why you will get the most benefit from the work that you've done with me.

Finally, take your time and enjoy the process. If you do your homework with the focus and passion you'd put into planning a fun vacation, it's very possible that you will find your love at last within ninety days. When you complete your winning profile, choose the right dating website that fits your needs and hold on to your hat because you're going to take off fast. During this time, don't plan on taking up a new hobby, starting a new job, or setting new goals for the year. Give yourself the gift of focus and enjoy the process. After all, you are doing what most people only wish they could do—designing your own soulmate, lover, life partner, best friend, and love at last. Enjoy the ride!

Top 21 Dating Websites

In this report, I've included the most popular dating websites as well as those more specific to cultural, age, and religious beliefs. The larger and more popular websites like Match.com include these same cultural, age, and religious belief specifics as well, but if, for instance, your belief is very strong in one particular religion, culture, or age preference, the specific, overall smaller website may suit you better. For instance, many of my love clients who are Jewish have found much success on JDate.com, even though they were on Match.com as well. So you can do the same and join one large site like Match.com and one smaller, more specific dating site if you find one that applies to you.

One word of caution to the person new to dating online: Join only one online dating site at a time. When you're a new member, you will be overwhelmed with requests to meet at the beginning because in the words of another client of mine, "You are fresh meat!" I suggest sticking to one site at first to prevent feeling overwhelmed and having the joy sucked out of your search efforts because the process begins to feel like work.

BlackPeopleMeet.com: The name says it all. This website is devoted to serving black singles. Although it has a smaller user base than other sites like Match.com and eHarmony.com, BlackPeopleMeet is a growing site exclusively for black and interracial dating.

BuddhistConnect.com: The largest Buddhist website for dating, social networking, and business networking.

BuddhistDatingService.com: "Find Nirvana with someone special" is this site's marketing speak. Once again, if being with an individual whose belief systems follow Buddhism is important to you, then this may be the right site.

BuddhistPassions.com: Largest free dating and social networking site for Buddhist singles.

Chemistry.com: This is a website devoted to LGBT (Lesbians, Gays, Bisexuals, and Transgenders) to help them find their love at last. This site does most of the work for you through strong personality matching results. Members are limited in their ability to search independently through profiles, so if you like to do the looking yourself, this may not be the site for you. But the site is focused on helping members find long-term love relationships.

ChristianMatchmaking.com: Do you want to join a dating site, but you're only interested in dating within the Christian faith? Then this is the place for you. It embraces all branches of Christianity, including Catholic, Greek Orthodox, and all of the different Protestant denominations. So if you're looking for someone whose beliefs are solely Christian in general or if you're looking for a specific type of Christian, this site would have a great selection of singles.

ChristianMingle.com: It's obvious from its name that this is a great site for Christian singles looking for other Christian singles. It's user-friendly with many interactive features like prayer requests, Bible study, and daily Bible verses. With a growing network of users and over 1 million members currently using the site every month, it is an obvious choice for Christian singles looking for a match.

CompatiblePartners.net: This is a website devoted to gays and lesbians who want to find the love of their lives. Brought to you by the people who brought you eHarmony.com, it also uses the scientific approach based on an intensive personality questionnaire for finding love.

eHarmony.com: This site's claim to fame is its scientific approach based on an intensive personality questionnaire for finding love. It also has a focus of Christian singles. It claims that ninety couples a day get married as a result of meeting here.

GreenSingles.com: Yes, it's a place where ecologically-minded singles can find like-minded, available, eco-conscious singles. This site is perfect for the person whose values and beliefs are highly driven by making the Earth a better, environmentally-healthier place.

JDate.com: This is the number one site for people of Jewish faith to meet other singles of Jewish faith. If finding a person of Jewish faith is one of your most important values, you'll have an easier time here finding someone available to you because of its wide selection.

JustSeniorSingles.com: This free dating site is devoted to fifty-plus mature singles. It also simplifies the online dating process to make it user-friendly, especially for some technology-challenged seniors.

LDSSingles.com: This website is specific to Mormon or Church of Latter Day Saints (LDS) singles.

Match.com: This was the site I used to find my love at last. It has been around the longest and is still the most popular of all the dating sites.

MeninLove.com: This is a local website for gay men to find casual meet-ups or for dating or finding the loves of their lives.

OKCupid.com: This free site connects LGBT singles for casual meet-ups or long-term love. As with any free site, you run the risk of meeting people who are less than committed in the search for happily ever after.

OurTime.com: Another popular fifty-plus website for mature singles. It also simplifies the online dating process to make it easy for some technology-challenged individuals.

PlentyofFish.com: POF (as it's referred to by enthusiasts) is one of the largest free websites devoted to finding the love of your life. Once again, this is a simple to operate website that has a phone-friendly app to appeal to our increasing appetite for anything mobile.

SeniorPeopleMeet.com: This website is for a massively growing segment of our population that is looking for that second or third chance at love that focuses on singles over fifty. A few of its unique features include an easy-to-navigate website, audio and video messaging, and daily suggestions based on your search criteria.

SingleParentMeet.com: The name says it all—it's a place that focuses on singles with kids, and as the statistics show, that is a growing segment of the dating world. It takes one possible negative disclosure out of the looking process by addressing it upfront. My husband Jim shared with me that in his dating experience in the Silicon Valley area of California, disclosing that you have children was a huge issue for some singles. So I can see the value of the approach this website takes. Now the only thing to address is the question of how many kids and how old.

Zoosk.com: This is the dating site for the new age of dating, syncing seamlessly with social media and mobile devices. Its claim to fame is its unique behavioral matchmaking capability that improves as you use its website, the theory being that the more you use it, the more likely you'll be to find exactly what you're looking for in a match.

Finding Love at Last

So what are you going to do?

Now that you've got the knowledge, what actions are you going to take? Are you going to pick up the phone and make a call or text? Are you going to send an email? What are your next actions that will bring you closer to finding your love at last?

Are you ready to put that big toe into the water? I challenge you to be brave, take a risk, and break out of your conditioned response of doing nothing. Too many people who have the answers do nothing about their situations. That's why they often mockingly call self-help books, "shelf-help."

How many people will buy and read a book on losing weight only to close the book and go on with their lives like they never learned the steps. You need to stand up! I mean now, stand up and do it. If it's a book on losing weight, go to the gym, clean out the junk food from your cupboard, or cook a healthy meal. But do something now!

I don't care what you do right this moment; whatever comes to mind first, do it! You'll begin the process and begin the momentum now. And once you've done that one thing, then do one more thing. The journey of a thousand miles begins with one step. Now is the time to take that step!

So stand up, and right now while standing, write in these next ten lines what you are going to do within the next ninety days. Don't worry if it isn't perfect. You can always adjust as you go forward. In the lines below, write out the top ten actions you commit to taking over the next ninety days. (For example, drop fifteen pounds, go to the gym three times a week, go to the orthodontist, update my profile on my dating website, etc.)

_____

_____

_____

_____

_____

_____

_____

_____

_____

Now that you know that the foundation of any relationship—especially with your love at last—is first knowing yourself, you must first know those values and beliefs that you hold dear in your life.

When you know who you are and what is important to you, only then can you know who is right for you. In the process of Love by Design™, you take the most important parts of your Mr. or Mrs. Right and put them together to form your manifestation letter. This letter is the key to attracting your life partner and keeping you on track during your search process.

This manifestation letter is also key to avoiding that dreaded Mr. or Mrs. Wrong—the antithesis of what you're looking for in your life. Sometimes, Mr. and Mrs. Wrong are wolves in sheep's clothing, and by habit, you may have been attracted to their type for ages. But now you are prepared to fight off any attempts of these wolves to get into your life.

Finding where your soulmate is hiding is important to discover. If you're looking for an outdoors type, you'll be more likely to find him or her at an REI store or shooting range rather than at an art museum. And if you opt into looking online, make sure you take what you've learned with you because without knowing who you are and who is right for you, the world of online dating can be very confusing and overwhelming.

Finally, once you are committed to the searching/attracting process, because you are so clear about what you want, this process will be easier and clearer than you've ever experienced. In fact, through the power of RAS (reticular activation system), you'll be eliminating suitors and never seeing them because you'll be engaging this superior focus. In most cases, you'll be doing more attracting than searching, and when you finally meet in person, you'll have the tools to eliminate the pretenders and pass on to the next level the real deals.

Finally, your elimination process will bring you *the one*. When you get to that point, it all becomes so easy and so clear that you wonder why it took you so long to find your love at last!

So by following this book's five simple steps, you'll attract your soulmate within ninety days and achieve what this book's title and subtitle promise.

Now that you've finished reading, I encourage you to contact me. Tell me what you liked or didn't like about this book so I can improve it for the next edition. More importantly, what issues in dating can I help you with? I will be thrilled to offer you a complimentary no-obligation thirty- to sixty-minute consultation, by phone, Skype, or in-person if geographically possible. To schedule a call, email or text me at:

Renee@FindingYourLoveatLast.com

424-281-0170

I wish you good luck and all the success life has to offer.

About Renée Michelle Gordon

Renée Michelle Gordon's heart is big enough to help you!

Renée was frustrated and sometimes just angry that she couldn't find the love of her life. And it wasn't because of a lack of interest or social life. She, like many people, just kept attracting the wrong person and repeating the same mistakes:

1. Find a guy.
2. Fall in love (or she thought).
3. Accept his proposal.
4. Wake up and smell the coffee.
5. Break it off just before the wedding.
6. Repeat steps 1 to 5 for nine times total!

With this type of track record, you would think Renée would have given up. But luckily, she was strongly influenced by the books she read and life lessons her father taught her. One of those lessons was that you can accomplish anything you want once you put your mind and heart into it.

So before she stumbled into wedding proposal number ten, she took time to learn more about the affairs of the heart, relationship matching, manifestation of goals, and interview techniques. She also was (and still is) mentored by one the world's greatest authorities on relationships, Dr. Ava Cadell. From all of this intense study and knowledge, she created what we now know as Renée's Top Five Love Attraction Strategies and she put those strategies into action for herself.

Renée, like many people, used the Internet as one of her tools for attraction and during a short three-month period, she attracted over 2,874 interested guys!

Now, for most people that would seem like a fantastic success. But her goal wasn't to be the most popular gal on the block. Her goal was to find the love of her life. So with a few adjustments to her process, she refined her approach and found the person of her dreams who has now been her husband for over fifteen years.

Renée is an author, professional speaker, and relationship coach. She has studied in the field of personal growth and achievement for over twenty years, and as a result, she has benefited by having the life of her dreams with the man of her dreams. Renée has helped more than 500 couples find their love at last and now is ready to help you do the same. Her mission is to eliminate the need for divorce and make the world a better place by helping people find love in their lives.

Renée lives with her dream husband Jim, their five dogs, forty-two exotic birds, five aquariums, and a giant Koi pond in Southern California. She has a passion for skiing and golfing and is an avid tennis player. She loves to travel and to cook gourmet dinners for her husband and all of her friends. She's an entrepreneur and philanthropist.

Having discovered how well her process worked, Renée now shares that process with couples worldwide through coaching, seminars, and now her book Finding Your Love at Last.

To learn more about Renée, visit her at:

www.FindingYourLoveatLast.com

www.ReneeMichelleGordon.com

www.LuvatLast.com

Retain
Renée Michelle Gordon to
Speak at Your Next Event

The team at Love at Last would proudly bring Renée Michelle Gordon to your live event. Renée can give a presentation or a workshop to fit your group's needs, whether your audience is five or five hundred.

The Love at Last process begins with finding out who you really are so you can best describe who is right for you through the Love by Design™ process for finding your Mr. or Mrs. Right. With Renée's help, you'll be able to determine who is the perfect person for you, and once and for all, identify the pretenders, the Mr. or Mrs. Wrongs, who keep popping up as love possibilities. Finally, you'll discover a way to find the right person so you won't be lonely, and instead, you can spend your life doing the things you love to do with your best friend. So don't settle, and don't repeat the mistakes of your past; let's begin your journey to love, made simple and to last!

For more information or to book an event, contact Renée at:

424-281-0170

Renee@FindingYourLoveatLast.com

www.FindingYourLoveatLast.com

www.ReneeMichelleGordon.com

www.LuvatLast.com